# STRAIGHT FROM
# YOUR GAY BEST FRIEND

# STRAIGHT FROM YOUR GAY BEST FRIEND

## THE STRAIGHT-UP TRUTH ABOUT RELATIONSHIPS, WORK, AND HAVING A FABULOUS LIFE

### TERRANCE DEAN

A BOLDEN BOOK

AGATE

CHICAGO

Printed in the United States.


Library of Congress Cataloging-in-Publication Data

Dean, Terrance.
 Straight from your gay best friend : the straight-up truth about relationships, work, and having a fabulous life / Terrance Dean.
     p. cm.
 Summary: "An advice guide for straight women from the vantage point of a gay man"--Provided by publisher.
 ISBN-13: 978-1-932841-56-5 (pbk.)
 ISBN-10: 1-932841-56-3 (pbk.)
 1. Man-woman relationships. 2. Mate selection. 3. Women--Conduct of life. I. Title.
 HQ801.D4355 2010
 646.7'7082--dc22
                          2010030201



10  11 12  13  14              10  9  8  7  6  5  4  3  2  1

Bolden is an imprint of Agate Publishing. Agate books are available in bulk at discount prices. For more information, go to agatepublishing.com.

*For my fabulous Divas, who make me so much better:*
*Monique Johnson, Chris Beal, Tonya Tait, Karen Johnson,*
*Alfreda Dean-Taylor, Cynthia Dean, Ailene Torres,*
*Toni Blackmon, Tamara Francois, Lydia Andrews,*
*Shirita Hightower, Felisha Booker,*
*Yona Deshommes, and Makeda Smith*

# Contents

# Chapter 1

# Get It Together: If It Don't Fit, Don't Force It

I was at a book signing in Detroit promoting my book *Hiding in Hip Hop* when I happened to encounter a beautiful woman. Rachel" was young, in her early twenties. She walked into the bookstore flustered. Actually, she was looking a mess. Her hair was all over the place. Her eyes were bloodshot. Her basic black skirt was wrinkled. Her black scuffed flats were just that—*flat*! I cringed. My gay fashion sense detector began wailing.

*Ring the alarm!*

Hurried and distracted, Rachel was not paying attention and stumbled directly into the table where I was signing copies of my book. She looked up at me, clearly disoriented. I asked if she was okay. At that moment, she snapped back to reality. Rachel refocused her attention on her surroundings and stated, "No, I am not okay."

I was glad she said that. If she'd said she was "fine," I would have had to pull her aside, do my godly duty as a gay man and tell her the truth: "Girl, you look a hot mess. What are you wearing? Have you looked in a mirror? Obviously your friends are not real friends, because they would *not* have let you come out looking the way you do!"

At any rate, I stopped what I was doing and gave her my undivided attention. I knew she needed someone to talk to.

I knew she needed me, a gay man, to talk to.

It was the way she'd answered and the look on her face. Rachel looked pitiful. She was wearing her emotions all over the cheap polyester sleeves of her bland blouse, and I could read them all. She was upset, angry, confused, and hurting.

No matter what she was going through, I would have been upset and crying too if I'd been wearing that catastrophe, designerless outfit. It was an eyesore.

Rachel began to tell me her story. She was on her lunch break, coming to the bookstore just to get away from the office. She was debating whether or not to call her soon-to-be-ex-boyfriend. He had informed her the night before that he was not ready for a long-term relationship, even though they had been dating for a year.

Now, in my mind, I was thinking, *Hint! When someone tells you he does not want to be in long-term relationship, let him go. There is no reason to hold on to someone who does not want to be with you.*

He'd told her he was still dealing with issues from his previous girlfriend and their child.

(*Hell, she should have been celebrating! A man with baby-momma drama? No way, no how.*)

I continued listening to her. Rachel was very distraught and up-set over the breakup. She did not want it to end. She wanted to work things out with him. She desperately wanted to speak with him. She was trying to decide whether to call him during her lunch break.

(*"Are you really as crazy as you look? You really want to call the man who dumped you last night because he wants to be with his child's mother and you knew the situation going into the relationship?"*)

One good Martini would have been great right about then. No, not for me. For her. Make that two Martinis. *Dry.*

She apologized for interrupting my book signing and imposing her issues on me. She started to turn away.

I could have left well enough alone. I could have let her go on her merry way. But the gay in me would not—could not—allow that. I owed it to my sister-in-need to be there for her. It would have been a disservice to my fellow gays to allow her to wallow in her misery (especially over a man) looking a hot mess as she trolloped through the streets with a horrid outfit on.

I hesitantly leaned over and touched her on the arm. "Girl, what are you doing tonight? We need to talk."

Over drinks that evening (Cosmos for her, Mojitos for me), Rachel told me how she had prayed for God to send her someone she could love. She wanted a spiritual relationship with a man, like the relationship she had with God himself. She wanted a man she could go to church with. A man she could pray with. A man she could have fun with. A man who loved her as much as she loved him. A man she could marry. She had waited for two years when this man finally showed up. And for the life of her, she could not understand why he now wanted to leave her.

I wanted to tell her, "Damn, girl, you are asking for a lot. You want too damn much!"

Rachel was now openly crying, and it tore my heart out. I've sat with so many of my girlfriends over bottles and bottles of wine (and rum, and gin…) as they cried their eyes out over a man. Oh, the pain. The heartache.

Yes, I have had my share of them, too. Men who walk all over you, stomp on your heart, and mistreat you while you give them your all-and-all. Putting them first. Then it simply ends and he walks away with some lame excuse. "It's me, not you." Or "I need to find myself. I need time to grow." Or "You deserve someone better." *Get a grip. Be a man!*

But I digress. My original intent was simply to let Rachel vent, because God knows she needed someone to listen to her, but I also knew she needed much more than that. She needed someone to set her straight.

"Rachel," I said, "Get real. Look at yourself. Even now, with all that mascara running down your eyes and snot coming out of your nose. You are gorgeous, girl. Don't you know you got it going on? Inside of you exists your fabulous self. That's right. *Your fabulous self.*"

Rachel put her drink down and looked at me.

"Honey, you have a *Diva* living inside of you, and you let this man come into your life and stuff her in a dark closet. Let me guess…you helped him upgrade his wardrobe, didn't you?"

She nodded yes.

"You taught him the difference between good carbs and bad carbs?"

She nodded yes again.

I crossed my arms across my chest. "And you got him to read *The Secret*?"

She looked at me. Surprised.

"I know, girl. I know."

I placed my hand on her top of hers.

"It's hard to let him go. And how he handled it was cold. It doesn't mean he's a jerk. He's just not ready for a woman like you."

I told her that sometimes we have to endure love lost in order to know our true worth and value. I told her how lucky she was he wanted to end it.

You should have seen her face. She looked at me like I'd reached across the table and snatched her purse.

I repeated myself.

"You are lucky," I said, "that the relationship only lasted a year, because there are some women who have been in relationships for five, ten, fifteen years, looking for an escape. There are women who have squandered their money, time, resources, and Spirit for far too long, because they are too afraid to leave."

She thought the two years she'd spent waiting for God to send her a man was long enough. (Hell, I know women who have waited longer. *Are still waiting*. But again, I digress.) Rachel was certain this *particular* man was meant for her because he showed up in her life at a time when she felt her spiritual walk was strong enough. (Hint: Just because you *feel* strong doesn't necessarily mean that you *are*. You have to wait on the Lord. Psalm 27:14. Read it.)

"You know something I've discovered?" I said. "The longer a woman has been in a relationship with a man, and the more she feels she's invested, the harder it is for her to let go, even when she knows she should. It's like letting go means admitting she made a mistake in the first place. She *did*—she settled for the wrong man—but that doesn't mean she should live with the mistake forever. She needs to forgive herself and move on. And that's exactly what you need to do, Rachel. Chalk up the year to a learning experience, and move the hell on."

I then proceeded to tell Rachel it was okay to feel the way she did. It was okay to cry and question why it had to be over.

But I told her to not let her Spirit die. I reminded her of scripture (2 Timothy 1:7): *For God has not given us the spirit of fear; but of power, and of love, and of a sound mind.*

I re-emphasized. When a man tells a woman he's not ready for a relationship, *she should believe him.* She should *not* try to change his mind.

"Why the hell would you want to hold on to something that just isn't working and is bringing you pain? Move the hell on, darling. There's someone out there ready for you, ready for a commitment," I told her. "Just be patient and you'll find him. The most important thing about relationships is, 'If it don't fit, don't force it. Just 'cause that's how you want it, don't mean it will be so.'" (Those are actually lyrics from an old song, but the advice is sound.)

Rachel smiled and thanked me.

I gave her a big hug.

And then, as she was leaving the bar, Rachel pulled out her cell phone and asked me if I thought she should call him.

Now, I know.

I know what you are thinking.

But grown folks are going to do what they want to do.

Sometimes, after talking yourself blue in the face, it's best to let people learn the hard way.

I smiled at her and told her not to call. She would be okay. Give it some time. He would call her. As we parted, I also told her, "Girl, I better not *see* you with that horrid outfit on again, looking like you got dressed in somebody's thrift store basement."

A few months later I got an e-mail from Rachel. She was extremely happy. She told me after reading my books, *Reclaim Your Power!* and *Hiding in Hip Hop,* she felt extremely inspired and powerful. She told me that she had moved on and she knew it was going to take some time, but she felt much better about herself.

More important, she realized she had not waited long enough. The man she needed was going to come, but this time, she'd recognize him. She wouldn't settle for less.

Whew.

All in a gay's day's work. (Sometimes I do admire myself for the wit my gayness has provided me. Yes, it is a gift.)

As I continued to tour across the country on various book signing events and speaking engagements, I encountered more women like Rachel. Also, many men. I am not sure if it is something in the water, or the carbs they are digesting, but these people seem to attract some of the most disturbing men I have ever heard of—immature, uneducated wannabe rappers who are over thirty years of age, living at home with their mothers, no car, no benefits, no job, no money, and no fashion sense.

Ugh!

The people I met were all desperate, asking what to do. Some of these women (and men) wanted advice on how to proceed in a relationship where they felt stuck. How could they get him to open up and talk to them? Why wasn't he motivated to do anything? How could they inspire and motivate these men to join them at church, engage in inspirational readings, or express their emotions?

But the number one question was always, how could they find and love the right man?

So, I grabbed my cocktail (no pun intended) and started doing small workshops with women (and men) to provide answers and solutions.

It was obvious they all needed a Gay Best Friend in their lives. *Every* woman needs one. Your Gay Best Friend has no ulterior motive. He is not trying to get into your pants or waiting for the moment he can bed you. He has no interest in sleeping with you. None whatsoever. And with no ulterior motive to complicate things, you can trust and believe his advice will be sincere and unbiased.

Who other than a Gay Best Friend is going to tell you the straight-up truth about your hair, clothing, and makeup? Yeah, your girlfriends may tell you what they think, but many times when you're going out with them, it's a competition for men. That smudge of lipstick, or your partial weave showing, or that outfit that doesn't quite fit right...well, your Gay Best Friend will tell you the truth about all of that, because he is not in competition with you. Your Gay Best Friend wants you to *win* this competition. He wants you always to look and feel your best. Best of all, you don't *ever* have to worry about him borrowing any of your fab clothing and not returning it.

That man you're sleeping with is no good? Your Gay Best Friend will tell you the truth. And guess what? You don't have to worry that a few weeks or months later, he will be sleeping with your ex (like those girlfriends who may be plotting and planning on how to get him after you). Remember what momma always said? "Don't tell your girlfriends about your man problems, especially how good or bad the sex is, because they will want to find out *how* good or bad the sex is." But your Gay Best Friend is not trying to sleep with your man. As a matter of fact, he will give you tips on how to sexually satisfy him or spice up the relationship.

You can talk candidly and openly with your Gay Best Friend, without judgments or filtering your conversation. There is nothing off-limits with your Gay Best Friend. There are no taboo topics and subjects with your Gay Best Friend. Talking about sex doesn't make him cringe. You can't go to your family or good girlfriends and speak candidly about sex: They may get offended by the topic. Your Gay Best Friend, however, will go there with you and allow you to share without any judgments.

Your Gay Best Friend is first and foremost a *man*. He knows, thinks, and feels as a man. He's familiar with the dating habits of men. Who better to tell you about what and how a man feels than your Gay Best Friend? (Some people tend to forget that gay men are still *men*. No, being gay doesn't make us any less manly. If you want insight into how a man thinks and feels emotionally, and how to get to his heart and into his head, your Gay Best Friend is the absolute best source.)

Finally, your Gay Best Friend is going to have your back. He will be there through thick and thin. We're not fair-weather friends; we're you're anchor, your rock. We stand with you through the storm. We won't run when times get hard, or when you're down and out. We won't talk about you behind your back. (No, we will do it to your face, because we love you unconditionally. We love you because you deserve to be loved.)

You are beautiful and wonderful. You are a Diva—divinely created for a greater purpose—and your Gay Best Friend will continuously remind you of that.

It is my duty—my gay tour of duty—to inform you that there are lots of options, possibilities, and resources to help create the life you deserve. *And* to find that man who is available and spiritually grounded. But Girl, we've got to work on *you* first.

Now, some women really do not know how to attract the right men because of their own insecurities, misconceptions, and self-doubts. They are so focused on fixing *him*, they don't think to look to themselves. That's where they'll find the answers to their own questions.

Yes, Peaches, sometimes the answer lies right in your own backyard. That horrible, despicable place you refuse to look because you have forgotten to tend to your own garden. You can't see the three-quarter-carat Harry Winston diamond perched in the middle of your weed-infested garden, so you look at the man, blaming him for your relationship not working.

As your new Gay Best Friend, your fiercest advocate, and your loudest voice to shout you back to your senses, I wrote this book. For you, the modern Diva woman (or Divo man).

Now, a Diva is a woman who knows what she wants and what she deserves. She knows she is number one—not two or three, but number *one*. She's not afraid to ask for what she knows she deserves, and nine times out of ten, she will get it. She's direct, pointed, and no-holds-barred in her conversation. Her use of language is sharp, like a scorpion's sting. She is not afraid to speak her mind. She's classy, sophisticated, cultured, and refined. Nothing is too good for her, and she knows it. People cater to her, and she doesn't have a problem with being catered to. She is adored, yet feared. People know not to cross her or get her upset.

A *Divo* is all that—in a man. He holds nothing back. He is confident and extremely sure of himself. He's the definition of class, sophistication, and refinement. He is not afraid to explore his cultured side and will challenge conventional wisdom of what machismo is. He will wear, dine, read, and do *anything he pleases,* for he knows it makes him a better, smarter, and more educated man. He knows nothing is too good for him.

Divas and Divos are everywhere. Think Patti LaBelle, Christina Aguilera, Mary J. Blige, Beyoncé, Lynn Whitfield, Cher, Bette Midler, Aretha Franklin, Jennifer Lopez, Angela Bassett, Tina Turner, Mariah Carey, and Janet Jackson. Think Kanye West, Sean "P. Diddy" Combs, Ne-Yo, Tyler Perry, and Sir Elton John.

This book is a guide for Divas (and Divos). A checklist for building the life (and attracting the man) you deserve. It provides hope, healing, and power to reclaim your destiny—a successful career, an abundant life, and a loving relationship with a man who is able to return the love, be nurturing, and able to express himself both emotionally and physically. You deserve and need to be loved as the whole person you already are.

Read this book. Put the information to good use. Think of it as a field guide to discovering hidden gems right in your own back yard. And these gems are *fierce.* Emeralds, rubies, and sapphires.

Take the book and share it with your friends: the ones who complain about their jobs and the places they work. The ones who feel life hasn't been fair and hasn't opened up doors for them to live in peace and with happiness. The ones who complain there are no good men or that they cannot find a man to love.

Let them know your fabulous new Gay Best Friend helped you pull yourself together, and he can help them, too.

Get ready for the journey and let yourself be free.

# Chapter 2

# Friend or Foe?
# Recognize Your Frenemies

*Friends—how many of us have them?*
*Friends—ones we can depend on.*

Remember those lyrics from the 1984 song by the rap group Whodini? (Am I dating myself?) Anyway, girl, they hit the nail on the head with that song. It was the anthem back in the day, and the lyrics still ring true today.

Your friends are the people with whom you have developed a long-term relationship, who are *always* there for you in the good and bad times. They love you despite your faults. You love them just the same. Your friends tell you the truth about yourself, and you appreciate them for it. You value their opinions, judgments, and advice. You know whatever they tell you, they are saying it out of love, not hate or jealousy or spite.

Friends matter. They help you become a better you. They inspire you, encourage you, and empower you.

You can be miles away, living in another state or country and you may not speak with your friend for days, months, or even years, but once you do communicate again, it's as if you'd just spoken earlier that same day. You can pick up the conversation right where you left off.

That, girl, is a *friend*.

It's important to have good friends in your life. They are just like your family members. They help shape and mold you into a better person. Especially if you have a fabulous friend who is like yourself. When you've got a friend who is fierce and fan-ta-bu-lous, watch out now! There is nothing you can't do.

But unfortunately I hear from too many women, "I don't have any female friends. I don't get along well with other women. They are jealous, bitter, and angry. They always start trouble. They are two-faced and backstabbing."

I am a firm believer that like attracts like. The energy you put out will attract the experiences you have in life. So when I hear women say those things, I look at them with a very cautious eye.

If those are the types of friends you are attracting, or the only types of people you have experienced, then obviously there is something about you that makes you attract those kinds of people into your life.

If you are a negative person and you have a negative attitude about things, then guess what? You will *always* attract negative experiences and negative people in your life.

Do me a favor, right now. Take inventory of the people in your life, especially your friends. What are the attributes you *like* about your friends? Make a whole column of the things you like about them. Take your time. Really think about it. List those positive qualities and get specific.

Throughout this book, I'll be giving you *a lot* of tasks. This is only the first. If you are going to have a fabulous life, surrounded by fabulous people, then it is my duty as your Gay Best Friend to make sure you get them done. It's going to take a lot of hard work to build your fabulous life, and if I don't make you look good, *I* won't look good. *Can I get a witness?*

Now, let's go back to your list of friends. This time, I need you to list the things you find disturbing about them, or that you don't particularly care for. Dig deep. Don't leave anything out. You need to do this.

I'll wait.

Finished? Good.

Are there things on your list like, "She gossips?" Or "I don't trust her farther than I can throw her?"

| Friend | Like | Don't Like |
|---|---|---|
| Shauna | Funny, smart, great company, fabulous taste in clothes, wonderful mom | Can be rude and catty. Can't keep a secret. Doesn't always listen. |
| | | |
| | | |

How about, "She always has something negative to say?"

What about, "She doesn't really talk about anything?"

This is a good one: "The conversation is always about her and her problems."

This one is *better*: "She thinks she is better than me."

Let me tell you something, darling. If any of those things are on your list, then you might need to take a good look at yourself. Your friends tend to be mirror images of you.

When you look at your two lists and there are more things on your "Don't Like" list than your "Like" list, then you really need to evaluate your friendship. Why are you keeping these people around, and how are they contributing to your well-being? If they are not contributing to making you a better person, or they leave you feeling drained and uninspired whenever they are around, then it's time to cut the cord of friendship. They are spiritual vampires, depleting and draining your energy. They are sucking the life out of you. Release them, and move on.

It doesn't serve you or them to allow someone in your life who doesn't leave you feeling wonderful, happy, inspired, or motivated. The sharing of positive energy between you and your friends should make you feel good. You should enjoy being around them, and not avoiding them when they call or come around. *You* have the power of your life. Do not allow negativity to engulf you, because if you do, you will become exactly like the friend whose company or friendship you don't enjoy.

I'll give you an example. If your friend gossips every time she calls you, or when you are together, then you are gossiping right along with her.

"But I just listen. I don't say anything!" You say.

Girl, stop it.

You know better than that.

If you are listening, you are contributing. Just because you don't say anything, that doesn't mean you're not involved. By listening to gossip, you are giving your friend a willing ear, and you are a participant.

Yes, you.

So, if you don't like the gossip, then tell your friend (if she really *is* your friend) that you are not interested in hearing it. Because if she is gossiping about others, trust and believe she is also gossiping about *you*.

If you *truly* don't like it when she gossips, then tell her.

But secretly, I'll bet at some level, you *like it*. That's why you keep answering the phone when she calls. Why wouldn't you? Girl, it's because she has the latest and juiciest information. She always knows what's happening with whom, when, and where. She is your sleuth. Because of her, you know when anything goes down, especially with someone you are close to. She knows how to get the information to you…quick, fast, and in a hurry.

If you want to have a fabulous life filled with joy, peace, happiness, and love, you need to surround yourself with those who will bring those things into your life. You've got to surround yourself with people who will help you grow into the fabulous Diva you are. People who are nurturing, inspiring, uplifting, and who encourage you to live out your dreams. People who will not try to bring you down, or nitpick at your dreams. People who are motivators and your biggest cheerleaders. They say things like, "Girl, go for it. You can do it." Or "Honey, you are smart and intelligent, so why *couldn't* you do it?"

Unfortunately, not everyone wants to see you do well or live your dream. They are dream-stealers, and they are probably already in your circle.

They are your frenemies.

Yes, a friend *and* enemy all in one. You might not know she is an enemy because she smiles to your face, but there she is, secretly hoping and wishing that you will fail at whatever you're doing. Of course you don't see her as an enemy. You wouldn't *knowingly* associate with someone who is plotting your demise. No, she *seems* to be your friend. She infiltrates your life. And then, at just the right moment, she does something that makes you question her friendship.

It's like the lyrics from the hit song "Back Stabbers" by the R&B group the O'Jays:

> *They smile in your face, all the time they wanna take*
> *your place,*
> *The back stabbers (back stabbers).*

That is exactly what frenemies are doing. Waiting to stab you in the back.

Your frenemies don't want to see you get ahead. They don't want to see you succeed. Every time you bring up something you're doing or seeking to do to build a fabulous life, they're the ones who say, "Why are you doing that? I don't think you should be doing it. You know it's hard." Or "I wouldn't do that if I were you. It's going to be difficult." No matter how much you try to explain to them it's your dream, they try to squash it.

Damn haters!

I remember something my grandmother always told me when I was a young boy. She said, "Don't let the left shoe know what the right shoe is doing." For a long time I didn't know what she meant. But as I got older, I started to understand those words.

My grandmother was telling me that I shouldn't let my friends know everything I was up to. There are some things I need to keep to myself.

And ladies, I am telling you the same thing. Some things, you just have to keep to yourself. Your dreams and aspirations are not to be shared with everyone. Most definitely not with your fren-emies. *(Give not that which is holy unto the dogs, neither cast ye your pearls before swine, lest they trample them under their feet, and turn again and rend you.* Matthew 7:6.)

Many years ago, a very good friend of mine and a fabulous Diva, Toni Blackmon, told me, "Terrance, make a list of your top three friends who support, encourage, and love you no matter what. And whenever you have some wonderful news to share about your ac-complishments, those three friends are your go-to people. If for whatever reason you cannot reach any of your three friends, then go into the bathroom, stare into the mirror, and share the wonder-ful news with yourself."

To this very day, that is something I do. I have a list of my very close friends I can tell anything. They are my encouragers, cheer-leaders, and spiritual advisors. They help me to stay uplifted and inspired. I can count on them for anything.

But if I can't reach them to share any great news I've received, or I am excited about something new in my life, I look into the mirror and say it to myself.

I do this because I know about frenemies firsthand. I've had them in my life. They've smiled in my face when things were going great. But when something bad happened or didn't go my way, oh, they couldn't *wait* to share it with everyone. They couldn't wait to talk about me to others behind my back. Once I discovered what they were up to, I cut them off. I eliminated them from my life. Nobody needs people around who are sitting, waiting, wanting to hear bad news about your life and spreading ill will on your dreams and aspirations. GOODBYE! And good riddance.

It bothers me when I hear people tell me about the so-called friends in their life who don't support them.

"Cheryl" in Philadelphia spoke with me about her "good girl-friend."

"Terrance, we have been friends for over ten years," Cheryl told me. "I love her dearly. She is my girl, but she is so negative. Nothing is ever good enough for her. She always discourages me and tells me what I can't do. Sometimes I don't answer the phone because I don't want to hear her criticism."

I sat with my arms folded. I was ready to tell her to drop her friend. I could tell, however, that Cheryl wouldn't follow my advice. Their friendship was a bond almost like a sisterhood, and that is one of the most difficult friendships to end.

"When I told her I was going back to school to get my bachelor's degree, she was like, 'Why are you doing that? You are too old to be going back to school,'" Cheryl said.

I looked into her eyes and saw the sadness. She hadn't expected to hear that from her friend, her sister.

"I was so hurt. But you know what? It made me that much more determined to go and prove her wrong."

"Good for you," I said.

"But that's not all. Now that I've earned my degree, all she says now is how I think I'm better than her. She didn't even come to my graduation."

Cheryl went on to tell me that her good girlfriend had had a rough childhood. Her parents were not encouraging. *No one* had ever encouraged her to do anything. She struggled through life. She had two daughters and didn't have a good relationship with either of them. As a matter of fact, Cheryl was her only friend, because people didn't appreciate her negative, nasty comments. Cheryl was her sounding board—and her verbal punching bag.

Now, don't get me wrong. I felt sorry for her friend. But regardless of her background and what happened to her in her life, she had no right to be mean and spiteful to Cheryl.

It was time to let loose and give it to her straight.

I got the feeling Cheryl already knew what to do about her "good girlfriend." She just needed me, a good Gay Best Friend, to give her that extra push to allow her to say what she'd been wanting to tell her friend for a long time.

I took a deep breath, reached deep down inside, set my mouth filter to Gentle, and told Cheryl the truth.

"You don't need someone like that in your life," I said as I unfolded my arms. "Cheryl, you are obviously a wonderful woman. You're full of positivity. A friend who harbors that much hatred will only be a detriment to your success. Why would you allow someone to nip at your dream that way? I don't care *who* it is. No one deserves to be told what they can't do and why they can't do it. And on top of it all, she didn't even come to your graduation!? I'm sorry, girl, but…she is *not* your friend."

Cheryl nodded in agreement. A tear formed in her eye.

I could tell that Cheryl was hurt by her "friend's" actions.

"I'm not saying you have to end your friendship, but you need to be honest with her and tell her about herself," I said to Cheryl as I handed her a tissue. "Let her know how her negativity impacts you. Encourage her to change. Know that it will not happen overnight, but if you want to maintain your friendship with her, then you have to give her boundaries. If she keeps overstepping them, then it's time to let her go." Cheryl agreed and thanked me for the advice. I gave her a big hug and told her to be encouraged in her Spirit. "You are more powerful than you know," I said.

And those are the same words I want to say to you right now. Sister girl, you are powerful. You are amazing. Smart. Intelligent. Brilliantly designed. And most of all, fabulous!

I encourage you to *be* your greatness.

I dare you to do whatever it is you desire.

I'm here for you.

There is nothing like having a Gay Best Friend in your life, because I will make sure you are living your best life. I will keep you laughing, empowered, uplifted, and motivated.

I, as your Gay Best Friend, spread only love and joy. What kind of friend hates on you and doesn't uplift you? What joy is there in that? How does that serve you—or *me*?

Girl, you better let those folks *go* who are sitting and waiting to speak negatively about you and your situation. I will not tolerate it, and neither should you.

It takes too much energy to keep folks around who are hating on you. You and I, we don't have time for hate. Like Mary J. Blige sang in her hit song "Family Affair."

*Don't need no hateration.*

Now, let's go celebrate and live life to the fullest.

# Chapter 3

# Spirit:
# Your Number One Relationship

I grew up in Detroit, Michigan, and was raised by my grandmother, Pearl Williams. My mother, Blanche, was unable to care for me and my younger brothers and sister. She was a heroin addict and a prostitute. I know she loved us, but the drugs had a strong grip on my mother, and she was unable to hide from the lure of her addiction.

Grandma Pearl prayed daily and nightly for my mother's recovery. She was a God-fearing woman who loved the Lord. She knew with God and prayer, anything could be made possible. And part of her prayer was that my mother's children be taken care of and have a roof over their heads.

My two brothers, one sister, and I were brought into Grandma Pearl's home and raised as her own children. My grandmother said that anyone living in her house was going to attend church and love the Lord just as much as she did.

So, my introduction to church and God came at an early age. Each week I attended church services with Grandma Pearl or my Aunt Priscilla. My aunt and her husband had seven children of their own. I would spend the weekend at their home and on Sunday mornings, we would awaken at five in the morning to start preparing for church services.

Now, for those you who know anything about various faiths, I was raised in the Pentecostal church. Which meant women could not wear pants or makeup. There was no cursing or listening to secular music. After you were baptized, it was known and expected that you would receive the Holy Ghost, speak in tongues, and shout in church. And that's exactly what I experienced.

I found solace in church for a number of reasons.

One, I, like Grandma Pearl, prayed for my mother's recovery from drugs. I wanted a real home, a real relationship, and real love from my mother. I didn't want to fantasize about having a family like the imaginary family I dreamed of when I watched *The Brady Bunch*. To me, they were the perfect family. They had a father, mother, and brothers and sisters who lived together and had fun. I wanted that. So, I prayed every day that my mother would come home and take me and my brothers and sister to a big house in the suburbs where we would be a family. I prayed because that is what Grandma Pearl taught me to do in times of crisis, challenges, and obstacles.

*My mother's return never happened.*

Two, I loved being in church because I wanted what the preacher had. He was charismatic. He was engaging. He held everyone's attention, and he appeared to have a direct line of communication with God. Each week he emphatically preached how God told him to do something, or how God told him to say something. God communicated with the preacher, and I wanted to hear God's voice too. I wondered what his voice sounded like. Was it loud and booming? Was it scary and mysterious? I had no idea, but I prayed every night that God would speak to me. I would hide under the blankets in my room staring into the darkness, waiting for God's voice.

*I didn't hear anything.*

Three, my family had learned that my mother had contracted HIV and passed it along to my baby brother, Javonte. He was born with the virus. That was a huge blow to my family. It turned my world upside down. I didn't know what to think or what to do. We struggled as a family trying to figure out what AIDS was about. How would it affect my mother's life, as well as my baby brother? Who would be his primary caretaker? My grandmother certainly could not raise a baby with a fatal disease. It was agreed upon, finally, that my uncle Andrew and his wife, Catherine, would take him into their home and raise him.

In the midst of all this, I prayed and went to church seeking answers. But it seemed to me the more I prayed, the more devastation hit my family. None of my friends or other family members appeared to be dealing with tragedy after tragedy as I was. I questioned God. I asked, "Why me? Why was I born to my mother and had the family I did?"

*I wanted and needed answers.*

Last, I wanted to escape my life. When I was thirteen years old, I had been raped by an adult male. He was a neighbor of my cousin. I would spend the weekends at Uncle Andrew and Aunt Catherine's home with their five children. One weekend, the next-door neighbor was asked to babysit us while the adults went out to party. While I was in bed with my cousin, the neighbor climbed into bed between me and my cousin and raped us both at the same time.

I was devastated.

I didn't understand why this man had done this to me and my cousin.

I feigned sleep while he stroked and sucked my erection.

I hated that I was turned on by the experience.

I wanted it to be over.

That experience was the beginning of my questioning of my sexuality. I had never been with another man, nor had I thought about being with a man prior to that experience. Until then, I had only had feelings and attractions to women. I had girlfriends. But being raped by another man and getting an erection made me wonder.

I began to question who I was.

I prayed every night for God to give me some insights. I needed some answers.

Was I gay?

Did I do something to cause this man to do what he did to me?

After the second time I was raped by the neighbor, I buried my shame and hid behind a wall of hurt, pain, and agony. I wasn't sure how I would recover from this tragedy. I was a kid, still developing and coming into my own. I had been violated, and my innocence was stolen from me.

I told the adults in my family what he had done to me and my cousin. I told because that was what Grandma Pearl had taught me. But after I told, nothing happened. No one consoled me. No one talked with me about what had happened. Life went on as usual. It was if it had never happened.

That left me even more confused and angry.

I felt for a while that maybe I deserved what had happened to me. Maybe I brought it on myself and encouraged him to do what he did to me. No matter what, the experience stirred something within me, and I began to fantasize about being with other boys. I hated having those thoughts, but they persisted.

When I went to church to find solace, I only found the preacher's sermons about God's hatred of homosexuality. He preached emphatically that being gay was a sin. Being homosexual was an abomination. God turned away from men who slept with men. I was going to die and go to hell. I would burn in the lakes of fire forever because of my impure thoughts of being with another man.

Oh, I prayed, and prayed, and prayed. I didn't want to die and go to hell. I didn't want to be an abomination, and for God to turn away from me. So, I asked God to remove my impure thoughts and feelings.

I prayed hard and long. I didn't want to be a homosexual. I wanted to be perfect, as I saw the preacher.

It seemed the more I prayed, the more I found it difficult to fight the urges and thoughts stirring inside me.

I didn't want to be gay, so I dated more girls, hoping it would dissolve the feelings I had. I figured I was going through a phase in my life. My thoughts would subside and I would move on with my life. I would be straight. I would be like my friends, and be normal like everyone else—at least what I perceived as "normal."

I didn't tell anyone about the feelings and thoughts I had. There was no one to talk to. I couldn't go to Grandma Pearl. I felt she wouldn't understand, and I was afraid of disappointing her. I had no father, and my mother was out of my life. I didn't feel comfortable talking with my friends or other family members, because they joked and teased boys who were effeminate. I didn't want them to taunt and make fun of me. So, I bottled up my feelings and said nothing.

Yet despite everything I was going through in my life, including my mother selling her body and being on drugs and leaving us to be raised by Grandma Pearl, being raped by an older man, struggling with my sexuality, and trying to find my way as man coming into himself, I remained faithful and prayerful.

I leaned on my faith and talked to God every day. Each time I knelt down, I felt God's presence and energy. I knew he lived in me and I was his child. I knew that no matter what, God loved me, but I would have to learn how to love myself.

That would take years.

As I grew older and continued to struggle with my sexuality, the reality became apparent. There was no cure or magical pill to make my desires go away.

I stopped going to church. I felt as if God wasn't listening to my prayers. I felt I really was not worthy of God's love. Every time I went to church, I was reminded by the pastors, preachers, and ministers that I was an abomination. I was not worthy of God's Holy Spirit dwelling within me.

I went into a deep depression. I hated my life and myself. I contemplated suicide, and twice I actually attempted to end my life. The first time I took a handful of pills and hoped my life would end swiftly. (Fortunately, it didn't work. I just suffered a severe stomachache and dizziness.) The second time, I thought of taking another bottle of pills, but after the first futile attempt, I reasoned against it.

I continued to date men and women, but primarily I dated men. I never dated men and women at the same time, but I went back and forth, hoping I would get an answer. Moreover, I was looking for the *right woman* to fall in love with. I figured if the right woman came along, I would not have to worry about my desires for men any longer.

*That never happened.*

As a matter of fact, I came to realize that I preferred and desired to be with men. I was gay. I was not down-low, bisexual, or confused.

*I was gay.*

Spiraling downward fast and without any direction, I found solace in being alone. I didn't have anyone to talk or share with about what I was experiencing.

Then I got the most devastating news. My mother was dying.

There was nothing the doctors could do. It was only a matter of time before AIDS ravaged her body and she would no longer be on this earth. I cried. I screamed. I yelled. I didn't want my mother to leave me. I didn't want to be alone in the world without a mother.

At that darkest hour, I received the most amazing gift. I was fortunate to be able to go home and spend time with my mother. We laughed and talked, and for the first time I let down my guard. I let my mother into my heart and I saw her with new eyes. She was a wonderful mother. She was compassionate and caring. Despite what the drugs and disease had done to her, my mother loved her children. She wanted the best for us.

I thanked God for allowing me the opportunity to be with my mother. I got to hear her say she loved me. It was the first time I had ever heard my mother tell me she loved me. That was confirmation for me. Those words lifted my heart and eased my spirit.

A few months after my visit with my mother, I got a call from Grandma Pearl telling me that my mother had died. The pain hit me hard because I knew I would never see my mother again, or hear her voice. I went further into the darkness and hid behind the walls I had built to protect me, refusing to allow someone else to leave and abandon me.

Then I got another call. My baby brother, Javonte, had died.

I couldn't take it any longer. I felt as if God was punishing me. He was taking my family away from me and leaving me to suffer.

I didn't understand why God would allow me to experience so much hurt and pain, and I was just a young man.

But I soon got an even bigger blow. I received a call that my *other* brother, George, was in the hospital. He, also, had AIDS.

He was nineteen years old.

Our family later discovered that George had been sexually molested when he lived in a group home for boys between the ages of eleven and thirteen. The male attendants raped my brother and he never said anything. Not until he was in the hospital.

When I got that call, I felt as if I couldn't take it anymore. I couldn't bear the pain of losing another family member to this deadly disease. I believed—truly believed—that God was out to get me. For some reason, He was on a mission to teach me a lesson. To make me pay for something I had done. Perhaps it was because I was gay.

I mean, why wouldn't I think this? The pastors I'd heard growing up often said how God punished people who sinned against Him. His anger and wrath were swift; that was what I had heard my whole life.

Certainly, I thought, He was angry with me and punishing me.

No sooner than I found out my brother George had AIDS, a few days later he, too, was gone. He left this earth and I felt he left me too. My world was no longer upside down, but topsy-turvy, spinning without an axis, and crashing.

This was the third person in my family that I had to bury. I had no more tears. I was broken down. I was beaten up.

However, I still continued to pray. I wasn't going to church, but I kept praying, asking God to show and lead me in the direction of His will and purpose. I asked that the right people, spiritual teachers and elders, be brought into my life. I wanted and needed direction, and I asked for information and resources that would help me on my journey.

The wonder of being open and allowing yourself to receive information is seeing that manifest right before your eyes.

Books on spirituality became available to me through friends or my own discovery. Books such as *You'll See It When You Believe It* by Dr. Wayne Dyer, *Value in the Valley* by Iyanla Vanzant, *The Game of Life and How to Play It* by Florence Scovel Shinn, *Conversations With God* by Neale Donald Walsch, and *The Four Agreements* by Miguel Ruiz.

Those books changed my life.

Those books helped me to rediscover my purpose and God's plan for my life. They provided insights into my value, purpose, and worth in the world, for my community, family, and God. I began to rebuild my spiritual muscles.

Miraculously, events started happening that led me to people who helped me journey back to my Spirit and my greatness. I met a man by the name of Adeyemi Bandele. He was doing a lot of spiritual work with men in the Maryland/Washington, D.C. area. I connected with him and discovered that he was the husband of the best-selling author Iyanla Vanzant. Yes, *the* Iyanla Vanzant. I had studied her books, and she was a great inspiration for me. I was able to meet her in person and speak with her on several occasions about my journey and spiritual development. She encouraged me and let me know that God was the source of all things, and despite what I felt about myself, God loved me. He was the source of love, light, and happiness.

*He lived in me and all others.*

When Iyanla shared this with me, I felt renewed in my mind, body, and soul. I was excited to hear this wonderful message of love coming from a woman who mentored and spoke to millions of readers across the country. I had one-on-one access to her, and I knew it was God speaking through her.

Then, I started going back to church. I knew I needed to be fed by a minister who spoke of truth, and not of hatred and abomination. I found a church home at Abyssinian Baptist Church in Harlem, with the Rev. Dr. Calvin O. Butts, III. Under his tutelage, I discovered a God who is loving. A God who loves all His children and His creations. A God who, despite ourselves, continues to loves us. A God who doesn't keep a track of our wrongs, but gives us direction and assistance to be better, live better, and be human.

Re-learning this as an adult, I was able to take the steps I needed to love myself. I was able to take steps to forgive myself for beating myself up and allowing others to judge, condemn, and dictate my life. I was able to heal, move forward, and walk in God's glory and light, for the purpose He designed me.

Yes, I still struggled, because in my head I continued to hear the voices of the ministers of my past who had told me I wasn't a part of God's kingdom. Who had said I was vile, impure, and disgusting. It hurt to think of myself as such, and I'm not sure if those ministers knew it, but that was a form of mental abuse. Their sermons had affected my psyche and how I lived my life. When you hear someone say to you over and over again how unworthy you are, how disgusting and vile you are, you begin to believe it. Especially if they have scripture and information to back up their heresy.

Slowly and surely, I built my self-esteem. I became stronger and wiser. I continued reading books, attending church services, praying and communicating with God daily, and meeting spiritual leaders who assisted me on my journey. I began to realize my purpose, and why I was on this earth. I began to understand how God used people and how we interacted with one another. More important, I realized I was a spiritual being having a human experience. No one could take that away from me.

*No one could deny or define me any longer.*

I then began to have serious conversations with myself about myself and my sexuality. I had to accept and admit who I was, and no matter what, I was God's creation. In my imperfections, I was perfect. God did not make any mistakes—in me or any other person. His Spirit lives in each and every one of us, and God is engaged and experiences life on Earth through each of us.

*Thank God for individuality.*

Once I accepted who I was, and whom I belonged to, I began to have conversations with my friends, and family members. I had to be authentic with them, just as I had been with myself. It was time to tell them the truth.

Trust me, honesty was no easy feat. It had taken me more than twenty years to accept myself. Now I was going to the people in my life, those I loved, to tell them to accept me...in a *day*.

In a letter to two of my aunts, I revealed to them my sexuality. I was told by a cousin that my aunt Priscilla cried. She couldn't handle it. She considered me one of her sons, as I was raised with her boys.

I understood why she cried. She was the woman who had helped nurture my relationship with God in the church. She was the one who had made sure I had a spiritual and religious foundation. She didn't want anything to happen to me. She was afraid for me.

It took a lot of time for us to have an open conversation about my sexuality, but once the door opened, we talked all the time. She got a full understanding of what I had experienced in my life and helped me answer some questions about God and Spirit. As we grew, so did our bond. She let me know that she loved me unconditionally.

She continues to embrace me as one of her sons.

The rest of my family embraced me just as equally and lovingly. What I had feared was going to be a difficult obstacle was the greatest and most powerful moment in my life. My family was able to embrace me because I had first learned how to love myself. I had allowed God into my life, and with God's power, grace, and Spirit, nothing is impossible.

There have been many moments when I've wanted to give up and turn my back on my spirituality. I even researched other religions—Buddhism, Scientology, New Age, Lutheranism. Yet I found each faith defined the source of life, light, and love as something bigger than us. Something greater and something we all come from.

For me, that something greater was God.

I'd been speaking to Him my whole life. Finally, I could hear Him speaking back.

When I travel across the country speaking at various colleges, universities, and events, people often ask me how I overcame the challenges in my life. They want to know how I was able to find peace and happiness. Each time, I reply that my faith in God kept and sustained me. It was God's undying love that allowed me to love myself, my family, and my loved ones. If God, whom I cannot see, loves me unconditionally, then I surely can love those in my life whom I *can* see.

My road, and my journey, certainly has not been an easy one, yet God never counted me out. He never allowed me to fall so far that He knew I wouldn't be able to get up.

There's a saying, "God will not give you more than you can bear." I am a firm believer in that statement.

God knew me. He knows me better than I know myself. In order to use me for His purpose, He had to break me down and build me back up—stronger, wiser, smarter, more defiant. I had to be molded and shaped specifically for my purpose. I had to remember who I was, am, and will become.

*The same is happening to you.*

God is preparing you. Shaping you. Molding you. Using you.

You may not be able to see it now, but in due time, everything will be revealed to you. Your purpose and journey will become so clear and so evident, nothing will be able to stop you from reaching and obtaining your goals.

I am your Gay Best Friend. I am here to tell you, girl, that we are *all* divinely created to serve, assist, help, and elevate one another. Each of us has been given specific talents and gifts that allow us to be of service to our families, our communities, and our world.

When it is your time, you will know. There will be no denying it. Your power, grace, and strength will resonate so brightly, it will be impossible for anyone to ignore.

It is important for you to know that God works with each of us in our own time. Some of us move faster than others, while many of us need extra special care and loving. We cannot compare our journey to another person's. We cannot compare where we are on our journey to where another is.

It is important that you stay focused on you, developing and nurturing yourself and God's Spirit within you. That is the most important relationship in your life. Your whole, fabulous, glorious life.

Yes, God does love you.

God is the source of all things, far and wide, big and small.

God will grant all your desires.

He will see you through the storm.

He will guide you and lift you when you fall.

All you have to do is let go and let God!

# Chapter 4

# Love Yourself: If You Don't, Who Will?

I know you would love a good romantic getaway. Of course I do. I'm your Gay Best Friend. I am supposed to know these things.

Let me tell you a love story.

This is the story of a man named Londell, who was in madly in love with a woman name Dedra.

When Londell met Dedra they were instantly attracted to one another. They were crazy about each other. It was a whirlwind relationship. They spent a lot of time together, and before he knew it, Londell was in love with Dedra. He had found the woman he could give his love to.

Dedra was everything Londell had ever wanted in a woman. She was beautiful, smart, and funny. She had an engaging personality. Dedra was a great conversationalist—not shy at all. No matter where they went, people loved talking to her. She was Londell's friend, lover, woman, and most important, the woman he had given his heart to.

Londell found it easy and comfortable talking with Dedra, and he told her *everything* about himself. He wanted her to know it all, because he knew she was going to be the woman he would spend the rest of his life with. In turn, Dedra opened up and told Londell everything about herself. Londell knew her background—where she grew up and where she went to high school and college, although she didn't finish. She had worked the majority of her life. She had a supportive and loving family.

Londell grew to love her more and more each day. He felt he had found his soul mate.

Dedra confessed to Londell that while growing up, she had been overweight. She had grown tired of the teasing from neighborhood kids, so she decided to lose the weight—and she did. She became active in sports while in high school, developing the most amazing athletic body Londell had ever seen on a woman. She was built like a brick house.

For some odd reason, however, Dedra was uncomfortable in her skin.

Men and women constantly gawked and complimented her body, and yet, although she knew she had an amazing body, she didn't want the attention that came with it.

Also, Dedra is dark-skinned. Not *very* dark, but dark-skinned. And she always called herself "black and ugly"—something that friends and people in her family had called her when she was younger. And now, without fail, whenever she was in a bad mood, upset, or disappointed, she would remind herself out loud how "black and ugly" she was.

She couldn't understand why anyone, especially Londell, would be attracted to her.

Dedra complained a lot about her physical and emotional self. Over the years, she came to dislike everything about herself. No matter how much Londell tried to reinforce her beauty, both inner and outer, she was not able or willing to hear him.

When she went to her pity party and started complaining about herself, Londell steadfastly refused to listen. He didn't see what Dedra saw. He saw, instead, her beauty, pure and untainted. He saw her heart and soul. He saw her brilliance in the conversations they had. He saw the love she had for her family when they were in need.

He saw nothing but good in everything she did.

After a year of dating, they decided to move in together.

Now, when you live with someone, it's *totally* different than before when you had separate apartments. Back then, you could just go home and have your own me time.

For Londell, living with Dedra became a full-time job nurturing her, trying to heal the wounds of her self-doubt. He slowly but surely became her counselor and therapist. He became her baggage carrier—and those bags were very heavy.

Despite it all, he still loved her more than she could imagine.

And yet, Dedra doubted Londell's love. She questioned why he loved her. She wanted to know what was so special about her. What qualities she had that kept him there with her.

Nothing Londell said or did was ever enough to convince her.

No matter how much money he spent or undivided time he gave her, no matter how many sacrifices he made, or hugs, kisses, or simple "I just love you because you are you" statements, Dedra never came around. She refused to allow him to love her.

Eventually, Dedra confessed to Londell that she didn't love herself. She didn't like who she was.

Unfortunately, Dedra had been damaged for a long, long time. The only person who could undo the damage was her. Dedra was the only one who could stop the voices in her head that told her she was dark, ugly, not worthy, not good enough, and stupid.

Londell tried and tried hard, ladies. He tried to love her enough for the both of them, but he simply couldn't. He was *drained*. There wasn't enough love in him (maybe even in the whole world) to make her see how much he loved her. He wanted her to know so desperately and so badly, that he had begun to neglect his own life to try and fix hers.

Let me tell you something.

Two unhealthy people trying to create a healthy relationship will not work. I know that for certain. I've been there, done that, and learned my lesson, girlfriend.

Now, when Londell told me what was going on, I knew he had a decision to make, and I told him so. "You either love yourself enough to let her go, or you spend the rest of your life trying to convince her how much you love her. You are not her therapist. You are not her counselor. You are her *man*. Get her in therapy, or you must leave the relationship. Otherwise you will find yourself resenting her and yourself."

Well, after *another* year of living together, Londell had finally had enough. He told Dedra that as much as he loved her, he was simply tired of trying to convince her of how much he did. He was becoming angry and bitter because she would not believe him.

Londell told her that he wanted her to be and have the best, and recommended a few therapists. He then ended the relationship and left. He left because he loved her so very much.

And as the saying goes, "If you love someone set them free. If they come back to you, they're yours. If not, it was never meant to be."

It is absolutely impossible to find and love a good spiritual man if you do not love yourself. If you cannot love you, then how can you expect a man to do it?

If you do not love *all* of you, which includes the things you *do not like about yourself*, a man will not be able to love you either.

With my group, Men's Empowerment, Inc., I have had open discussions about love. On countless occasions, I have heard men say it's hard to be in a relationship with a woman who doesn't love herself. These men have shared openly and honestly their views and opinions on the issue.

What I and so many other men have shared is that when a woman is down and hard on herself, it becomes difficult for the man to stay in the relationship. A man will do all that he can to make her feel appreciated, but it's never enough.

Traveling across the country and speaking at various events, I have met many women who do not appreciate their beauty and greatness. I listen to them complain about everything from their weight to their boyfriends. It really bothers me that these, and many other women, are willing to put themselves down.

Even if you are not doing it in public, you are doing it in the privacy of your own home.

Girl, don't sit there like you don't.

You stand in front of the mirror picking yourself apart, don't you? Well, at least some of the time.

You look at magazines and at videos and compare yourself to these women in their airbrushed, made-up, back-lit perfection.

You blast yourself for not being smaller, taller, prettier, smarter, and stronger.

You have too many flaws and you point out all the things that are wrong with you.

When people give you compliments on the weight you've lost, you reply that you've got more weight to lose.

When someone tells you you're wearing a nice outfit, you say, "This old thing?"

You don't accept the compliments graciously.

You find loving yourself difficult.

———————

I was in Detroit a couple of years ago speaking and hosting a workshop for women at the Shrine of the Black Madonna. It was a very nice crowd of women, listening intently.

The event went smoothly, for the most part, and the majority of women there were very receptive to the information I shared with them.

But there was one woman, "Brenda," who I, and most of the other women who were there, will never forget.

Brenda was in a relationship with a man and looking for something she could do to make him love her. Brenda had read self-help and relationship books, attended workshops on love, and gotten advice from friends. She said that she had searched all over for an answer. Still, she could not find one.

It was not until Brenda was sitting in my workshop that something clicked for her. She heard something that no one else had said to her. Something finally registered in her psyche that helped her to see what the problem was.

She discovered that she had not loved herself.

(You see what a good Gay Best Friend can do for you?)

Although her boyfriend was a great lover, friend, and companion, Brenda had always found fault with herself. She questioned and doubted why he was in the relationship with her. Brenda felt she was not pretty enough, and she told all of us in attendance that her nose was too big and her hips were too wide. She said she could stand to lose a few more pounds. She didn't think she was smart enough. She'd dropped out of college without getting her degree, and yet she held a prominent position in her company.

Brenda went on and on about all the things she didn't like about herself. Quite frankly, there was nothing visibly unattractive about her. Even the other women in the audience chimed in with compliments.

I told Brenda, "You have to love your thighs, hair, nose, eyes, feet, butt, breasts, and even your stomach. You have to love all your little quirks that may be annoying or off-putting. Everything you may find fault with, you've got to learn to *love it*. Love *you*, completely and totally."

Spirit loves all of you, despite yourself.

Spirit loves you enough to continuously provide you with everything you need or want.

There are no minimum requirements for Spirit to love you. So, why can't you do the same for yourself?

It's because when you were younger, someone did or said something negative about you and you *believed it*. Without even knowing it at a conscious level, you have allowed someone *else's* opinion about you affect you for the rest of your life.

When you were just a little girl, someone made you feel inadequate somehow. The kids teased you about your hair, clothes, or figure. Someone told you that you were not worthy. Then you read articles in magazines that confirmed something was wrong with you. The programs you watched on television enforced the Hollywood standard of beauty. You tried to compete, but you struggled. You, again, surmised that something must be wrong with you.

You compare yourself constantly to everyone and every woman you meet.

Go ahead and admit it. Hell, I've even done it. (Well, not compared myself with other women, but other men.)

When your ex-boyfriend or some man you've dated is with another woman, you compare yourself to her. You ask yourself, "What is it that she has that I don't? What makes him want to love her and not me?"

Stop doing that. Right now, stop it.

Stop comparing yourself. Stop making yourself wrong. You hold all the power over your own life. Stop giving it away to others. Stop allowing them to dictate how and what you should look and be like.

Love you. The total package you are. Love it graciously and mercifully.

God created you out of His image—His imagination. You are a gift from the original source of love, so go back to the source for your inspiration.

*Beloved, let us love one another: for love is of God...* (1 John 4:7).

*God is love; and he that dwelleth in love dwelleth in God, and God in him.* (1 John 4:16).

Forgetting to love yourself—or never learning to in the first place—can have life-shattering consequences.

I remember when my aunt told me that she and my uncle were getting a divorce. I was devastated. They had been together since she was a teenager. That's over thirty years, and he was the only man that she'd known.

When we talked about the divorce, I could hear in her voice that it was final. She was tired. Tired of beating up on herself, and tired of trying to hold on to something that was unfortunately coming to an end.

She told me that she had completely let herself go in the marriage. She was not blaming herself, but realized that she had *stopped loving herself* and dedicated her life to her husband and children. Ultimately she neglected herself.

She was a housewife, one of the most difficult jobs in the world. She gave my uncle seven beautiful, wonderful, and smart children. She labored for them day in and day out. She had her hands full all the time.

When my uncle announced he was leaving her, she was crushed. My uncle was leaving her for another woman. My aunt said she felt like her life was ending.

She didn't want the marriage to end. She wanted to work things out. She wanted to know what she could do to keep their marriage alive, but it was too late. My uncle had already decided he was moving on.

I have never experienced divorce or the end of a years-long relationship, but I could sympathize with my aunt. I listened to her because it was therapeutic for both of us to talk about what happened.

Once it finally hit my aunt that the marriage was truly over, she let her husband go. She let him go be with the other woman. She let him out of her system.

She let him go because she realized she needed to love herself, and in order to do that, she had to release him.

When she told me later that she learned to love herself again, I smiled to myself. It was a wonderful lesson for her. She said she now understands how people can lose themselves when they don't love themselves. She thought her life was *his* life. She thought she could not function or live without him. But now my aunt has created more of a life on her own, and, more important, she got herself back.

Like Jill Scott sings in her hit song "Golden," my aunt is living her life like it's golden.

After hearing my aunt's story, I wanted to share it with every woman. No matter what you think or have experienced, no matter what you've heard and internalized, no matter how hard it is to get there, you must love yourself.

You must love yourself even when your family requires your time and energy.

You must put yourself first.

You must love yourself even when you think you may never meet the man of your dreams.

A lot of women I meet at workshops will introduce themselves and then immediately begin tearing themselves down. It's automatic. Many women do it before they allow anyone else to do it. These women focus on negative things and never promote the positive.

After I listen to them tear themselves down, I always ask, "How do you feel after telling me about all your faults? How do you feel now that you let me know what's wrong with you?"

Usually I get blank stares.

I encourage them—and I want to encourage you—to tell me all the *wonderful* things. I want to hear all the great and exciting things that you never tell anyone.

It takes time and practice to start saying all the awesome things you have accomplished or are creating. Give yourself that time. Make yourself practice.

Take the time to tell yourself each morning, afternoon and evening how much you love yourself, no matter what you feel and others think about you.

This exercise is easy and can take anywhere from five to fifteen minutes. Go into your bathroom, or wherever you have a mirror, and stare at yourself. Look at your eyes, nose, mouth, and ears. Admire the delicate and intricate unique make-up of you. Smile, show your teeth. Then say, "I love you." Declare it boldly. Say it proud and loud. "I love you!" Keep repeating it over and over again. As you repeat this mantra, notice how your body feels. Notice how your body responds. Every molecule and cell will react and a wonderful feeling will wash over you. That is the power of Spirit. Doesn't it feel great? Doesn't it feel wonderful?

Girl, I am telling you, when you love you like no other, watch as Spirit brings more love into your life—like, eventually, the man you deserve.

# Chapter 5

# Get Some Me Time: Not Some Him and Some Her, Just a Little Me Time

*I need some me time*
*Not some you and some I*
*Just some me time, oh—*
*I need some she time*
*Not some him and some her*
*Just a little bit of free time*

—Heather Headley, "Me Time"

There is nothing like spending some quality time alone. Especially after a long day at work. You get to unwind, de-stress, and relax. There is no one around asking you any questions, nagging you, or asking you to do something. It is time just for you.

Have you ever seen a woman who looks like she is carrying the weight of the world on her shoulders? I have. More than once. She is run-down, bags under her eyes, hair all over the top of her head, wig sitting lopsided, clothes disheveled. She is just a mess. I want to run over, grab her, and say, "Girl, what's *wrong* with you? Has life really been that mean?" But I don't, because I know an angry and stressed woman will whip her head toward me, put her hands on her hips, start rolling her neck, and read me the riot act.

Well, anyway, you're not that woman, I'm sure.

But I'm here to tell you, as your Gay Best Friend, there is *no* excuse for you ever to get that bogged down and stressed. No reason to wear life's worries on your face, back, and legs. (For one thing, girl, doing that makes you look heavy and bloated!)

To alleviate the worry and stress padding around your problem areas, you've got to make some time for yourself.

That's right. Take time to be with yourself, just you.

Cooking, cleaning, and taking care of the family or running behind your man is not taking time for yourself. Making sure everyone else has what they need is not taking time for yourself. And trying to please and make everyone else happy is *definitely* not taking time for yourself.

When you do for *you*, all others take second, third—hell, even fourth place. You have to prioritize. You belong at the top of your list. And to do that, you must schedule time in your day that is just for you.

Set aside thirty, sixty, ninety, or a hundred and twenty minutes to do something only for you. Try sitting in a hot tub with your favorite oils and bubbles, with scented candles lit and soft music playing in the background. Make a weekly trip to the nail salon to get a manicure and pedicure. Perhaps you want to go the spa every other week and get a massage, facial treatment, or exfoliating service. Whatever it is you decide you need, *do it,* girlfriend.

And don't feel guilty for it.

Many women feel guilty for taking time to do for themselves. They feel that being good to themselves takes time away from their friends, children, family, and husbands or boyfriends, who *desperately* need them. They feel that, somehow, things will fall apart if they go away for a half an hour, and their loved ones will not be able to function without them.

Those loved ones might think so as well. Trust me, once you start making time for yourself, your man, children, family, and friends will all start to make you feel like you are ignoring them. It just may work, too—at least in the beginning. You take a few minutes to open a book (maybe *this one!)* or listen to your music with your headphones. Close your eyes and you just might hear yourself starting to make apologies, trying to explain that you just need five, ten, or fifteen minutes to gather your bearings.

Girl!

Stop it!

You don't owe anyone an explanation when you are caring for and loving yourself. You don't have to explain why you need to regroup, refresh, and reassess. The only person you owe an explanation or apology to is yourself.

If they keep bugging you, then you borrow Heather Headley's line: "I need some me time. Not some you and some I, just a little me time. That's all."

Heather obviously knows the importance of taking time for herself, and she sang it for all the women who feel the same way.

Let me tell you, sister, if you don't take time for yourself, you will be wearing a new makeup line called "Stress." You will be donning a new dress by the designer "Worry" and fierce pumps by "Tired."

That is not a cute outfit. It's hideous.

No, really. It's true.

People will stare at you and say, "She really let herself go. She looks atrocious."

Keep the receipts and take all that stuff back, because you don't need it.

Get a full refund and get you some happiness. Joy. Peace. Love. Sanity.

"But how can I step away and take time for myself?" You ask. "I have a family and they need me. My man expects a hot meal when he comes home. I've got to maintain the home, and that is a job in and of itself."

First off, I'll say it. Women have the hardest job in the world, especially if they are raising a family. My gosh! That is a full-time job with an exorbitant amount of overtime. You get your kids up and ready. Make breakfast. Walk or drive them to school. Then go straight back home to clean up behind them, constantly washing and cooking. Then you have to go back to school and pick them up, run errands, help them with homework, talk with them, sign permission slips, feed them, get them ready for bed, and start all over again the next day.

And in between all of *that* you have to be a wife, girlfriend, lover, and mate to your man. Whew! Oh, honey, I know I am leaving some things off the list, but you get my drift. Your work never ends.

So, yes, it's hard for women with a family to have a personal life. It's hard to create a life of your own because you want to live for your family. And rightly so. You want the best of things for your children, and you want them to be well-rounded. You give everything you have to make sure your children are happy.

You won't get an argument out of me. I totally understand.

Look. My grandmother gave up her retirement to care for me. My mother succumbed to drugs, and not too long after, I was on the doorstep of my grandmother's home, along with my little brothers and sister, and a slew of cousins soon followed. She stopped her life to care for all of us.

One of my aunts, whom I spoke of in the last chapter, has seven children. She was married and had to maintain an entire household of nine people, including herself. Whenever I went to her home, I couldn't imagine that many people in one house. Yet, my aunt managed. She created a daily routine that had her going from five in the morning to eleven at night.

Many of my female friends have families. I am often in awe of how they do it all, including working a full-time job. These sisters work it out and make it happen, but one constant complaint I hear is, "Can I get a *break*?"

Yes, they want some time alone. Some time for themselves. And for once, to not have their children up in their faces asking a million questions, or someplace they need to be at a certain time.

Here's my advice, Diva.

I recommend getting some additional help. You know, a nanny or housekeeper. Someone to come in and help you with the day-to-day things you become overwhelmed with.

Oh, stop yelling at me. I know everyone can't afford to hire a nanny or housekeeper. This piece of advice is for those of you who have really considered it, or have said it at one time or another, and can afford to hire some additional help.

There is *nothing wrong* with hiring someone to come in once, twice, or three times a week to help you with the house chores while you focus on the kids or take a good few hours for yourself to relax. If you can get a nanny, that would be even more helpful, especially if you are a working mom. The nanny can pick up the kids from school, make sure they do their homework, cook for them. And when *you* get home, you can sit and *talk* with your kids about their day and other events.

Hiring additional help does not make you a bad person, or someone who is disorganized and can't maintain her home. No, it does not mean that at all. There isn't a person, especially another woman, who would tell you that you are a bad parent for hiring someone to help you around the house. (If she's smart, she's will ask if they can use your person for *herself.*)

Now, if you *can't* afford a nanny or housekeeper, you can enlist a family member, good friend, or even one of your younger nieces or nephews to babysit. Yes, I know it might be a stretch, but if you approach them lovingly and explain to them that you want to take at least a few hours to gather yourself, go the mall, or soak in the tub, I don't think most of them would mind taking the kids off your hands.

I do know that your nieces and nephews also wouldn't mind if you offered to pay them for their services.

Young people today are always looking for ways to earn some extra cash. It is a great incentive if you offer (depending on their age) at least ten dollars an hour.

You can even get your husband or boyfriend to sit with the kids while you detoxify from the stresses of life. They are his children too. He can sit with them while you take some time for yourself.

I know what you're thinking. Some men wouldn't know what to do after thirty minutes. He will forget to feed them. He won't make them go to bed on time. He will give them their video games or put them in front of the television to preoccupy them.

As long as they don't tear down the house, girl, go and *enjoy yourself.*

If you are a single working woman, or if you have a man and the two of you have no children, I *still* recommend taking time for you. You still need those moments to pamper and take care of yourself. And you know what I suggest?

Shopping therapy. Yes, yes, yes! Who doesn't love going to the mall and shopping for clothes, shoes, purses, and makeup? That is the best relaxer and most pleasurable experience you can have sometimes (especially when you score a great sale or discount).

On the weekends, I suggest you gather the girls and have a spa day. Get your girlfriends. (The real ones—not those frenemies.) Go treat yourselves to massages, manicures, and pedicures. Get a facial scrub. Let someone pamper you. Then afterwards you can grab a late lunch or early dinner at your favorite restaurant.

Doesn't that sound fabulous? Yes, I know it does. And you deserve it.

If you can pamper, cater to, and love yourself, the stresses of life will not seem as monumental, because you'll know how to relieve all the stresses and worries that come your way. You, relaxed and rested and revved up, will wear a smile so wide and bright it will attract men from near to far. Your attitude will change. You will glow—happy, carefree, and light. You'll find yourself singing and dancing while others around you are looking sad and miserable.

Honey, you got to *live* life and not let it live you.

When I was home visiting in Detroit, my cousin, Alfreda, who I call my Muse, looked really tired. I heard it in her voice when I spoke with her on the phone before I went to visit her at her home.

Alfreda is married to a wonderful man named Chris, and they have three adorable, beautiful daughters. Oh my gosh, they are the smartest and liveliest little girls. I love visiting them because they love to talk with me, and they dance for me. I have a ball every time I visit.

However, my cousin, Alfreda, wasn't dressed fly and fabulous like I know her to be. Her hair was down and not in one of her unusual Detroit hairstyles. (Let me tell you, Detroit women don't play when it comes to their hair. The colors, styles, and accessories on top of their heads clearly make Detroit the hair capitol).

Alfreda is a stay-at-home mom. She has her hands full with those three young girls, constantly cleaning behind them, helping her eldest daughter with her homework, changing diapers, potty training, and talking with them. On top of all that, she cooks three meals a day for her children and makes sure her husband's dinner is ready when he comes in from a long day at work.

She does the grocery shopping, doctors' appointments, parent-teacher conferences, after-school programs, and she even goes to school at Wayne State University, where she is in her third year. I always tell her how proud of her I am. For her to have a family and go to school, that is amazing. She is a superwoman.

She is fabulous.

She is a Diva!

Well, during my visit she mentioned that she wanted to attend a concert at the end of the month, which happened to be around her birthday. Every time we spoke, she brought up the concert and how she really wanted to go.

I secretly purchased two tickets and presented her with them as a birthday gift. I did it not only because she deserved to go and enjoy herself, but also because she really needed some time away from home.

My cousin was ecstatic. The smile on her face was priceless. It felt wonderful giving her those tickets and seeing her enthusiasm. I knew she was not only excited about attending the concert, but also to be doing something she could enjoy for herself, without the kids, for a few hours. Don't get me wrong, she loves her three little girls, and she goes above and beyond to make sure they are well taken care of, but a few hours to have fun, and dance? Yeah, she deserved it.

Alfreda decided she would take her husband to the concert with her. She wanted to have a night out on the town, just the two of them. She arranged for her older sister, Cynthia, to watch her daughters for the night, and Alfreda and her husband went to the concert and had dinner afterward.

Alfreda had the most amazing time. She bragged and talked about that concert, reliving it as if she was a young girl who'd gone to her first concert. I smiled as she gave me the blow-by-blow details of the event. I was happy she had a great time—some time just for her.

You see, my fabulous Divas, it can be the smallest and most intimate of things you can do to enjoy yourself. Find what makes you happy. Do the things that bring you joy and peace in your Spirit.

It can be as simple as closing your bedroom door and climbing in bed under the covers with lots of scented candles lit and a good book to keep you company.

Or you can find an event you want to attend. Maybe it's a movie you've heard good reviews about. Go! Have fun. Enjoy yourself.

Those hours of sanity will allow you to still your mind. They will do wonders for the glow that makes you shine as bright as the sun. And I need for you to shine if you're going to be my fabulous friend!

# Chapter 6

# Stimulate MENtally and Physically:
# From Manolos to MOMA

"You know, Terrance, for the life of me I can't figure out why the hell I can't find a man," a former colleague, "Asia," was telling me over lunch. "I have a good job. I'm educated and intelligent. I take care of myself, and I know I look good."

I wasn't going to say anything at first, because she was talking but not really asking, but I guess she must have seen me mentally rolling my eyes.

"What?" Asia asked, with *way* too much attitude in her voice. "You don't think I look good? You think that's the problem?"

Now, Asia, who runs her own department at a major record label, stands about five feet nine inches in her bare feet and is voluptuous, with a body that would make both Tyra Banks and Vivica A. Fox drop their heads in shame. But because she was asking me, I was gonna lay down the truth.

"Yeah, you got the face and the body, but girl, you sure as hell don't know what to do with them," I told her. "Someone needs to teach you how to *dress.*"

It was time for me to whip out my Lemon Drop glass and Tiffany crystal wand. It was time for me to tell her like it was. You should have seen the expression on her face. Her hand flew to her hips, and she gave me the girlfriend head-roll.

"I'll have you know I spend good money on my clothes..."

"Yeah," I interrupted her, "but it's not how *much* you're spending, it's what you're spending it *on*. If you want a man, you have to stop dressing like one."

I didn't mean her any harm, but I could tell she took it hard.

Here she was, having lunch, bemoaning the fact that men weren't talking to her, wearing an expensive two-piece dark gray business suit (pants, not skirt) with a silk blouse buttoned to the top and her long hair pulled into a librarian bun. I still shiver thinking about the entire get-up.

I mean, it was cute, but not for the environment she works in: Entertainment.

Even when Asia was *not* dressed in a suit, and just doing grocery shopping or going to the laundry, she was wearing sweatsuits, sneakers and ball caps.

HATE IT!

As her sworn Gay Best Friend, I told Asia the straight-up truth. I understood she worked in a male-dominated industry. I understood that she feared that if she did dress up, her male colleagues might not take her seriously and might be tempted to treat her like the women in music videos.

But I also told her that men like to see the curves of women. They like to see a woman being feminine. Men like a woman who can have on jeans (Ed Hardy, True Religion, or Antik) but dress them up with a nice blouse and shoes (Marc Jacobs, Prada, or Gucci). It's okay to wear sweatsuits, sneakers, and ball caps on occasion, but not as your everyday dress.

At first, Asia didn't agree with me. She didn't want to believe what I was saying to her. (Not one to toot my own horn, but I *am* her Gay Best Friend, and I *do* happen to know a little something about fashion and what a woman should be wearing.) So I suggested she ask the men and women around her department what they thought of her dress.

When she came back and told me what she'd discovered, I could tell Asia was shocked. The overall consensus was that she *did* dress like a boy. Quite often. They thought it would be nice to see her in something different, something more feminine. I held up my Manhattan on the rocks (we all want to feel like big fashionistas in the city).

Touché.

Mark one point for me.

A Gay Best Friend never fails.

Asia thought her intelligence and successful career were going to attract a man. Now, there is nothing wrong with being a smart and career-minded woman. A lot of men find that very attractive. However, you've got to combine your *looks* with your mind. I knew it was hard for Asia to admit to herself, but she had gotten caught up in her career and stopped presenting herself as a sexy, desirable woman. She wanted to fit into her environment and did not want to be seen as a sexual object.

Whew!

You, my little mutton chop, like Asia, are a *winner*. And as your Gay Best Friend, I won't let you dumb down, dress down, or *be* down. When you have a Gay Best Friend, that's your ace in the hole. Your trump card. He is your eyes, ears, and best accessory like your favorite Hermès bag, only with *attitude*. You need one to survive. Can't live without one.

———

Listen up, ladies. There is nothing wrong with putting on a little makeup, wearing a dress or skirt, and making it pop with some nice heels, either high or low.

There is also nothing wrong with getting your hair done regularly and pampering yourself.

You say you don't know who I'm talking about?

Oh, my little pudding pop, you see her every day. Some of you may even know her. She is your girlfriend, sister, colleague. Other girls talk about her behind her back and don't even offer to help her fix herself up. They ought to be ashamed of themselves. Laughing and pointing. Discussing her like she is an outcast sixth-grader with no fashion sense.

Okay, I admit, she does look painfully awkward and stiff with different blends of material and mix-matching designer brands.

But wait!

Some of those who are doing the gossiping are the ones who need a makeover. Just because they've got a man, they think they can stop putting effort into themselves? Some women actually think because they already got him, it gives them a license to stop dressing up?

Hold up!

A Diva doesn't stop making herself fabulous. She keeps on doing it. You can shake it up a little by doing different things. Don't get complacent and predictable with your hairstyle, makeup, or dress. Experiment with your sexiness. Check out the beauty books by *Essence* magazine, Sam Fine, and Lloyd Boston. Read *Cosmopolitan, Vogue, Marie Claire,* and *Redbook.* These are your fashion and makeup bibles. Every woman (and Gay Best Friend) should read them monthly. (If your Gay Best Friend is *not* reading them, you'd better make sure he is a true, card-carrying Gay Best Friend. What a disappointment if he isn't. Then he is useless to you.)

Back to your fabulous self.

Let's face it, men are visual creatures. I know a lot of women don't want to hear it, but yes, a man does want a woman who looks good. Sure, he wants a woman with intelligence and wit, but even more, he wants a woman he loves to look at and show off to his friends and family. He wants to be envied. He wants every man to want the woman he's got.

Ask a man what's the *first* thing he notices about a woman, and he will tell you about a physical attribute, like the butt or chest (men will be men, after all). Second, he may mention the way she is dressed. Third, her hair, makeup and nails. And fourth, her attitude and personality.

Point-blank, men are attracted to women who take care of themselves both physically *and* mentally.

Men like women who take the time to care for their physical well-being.

I come across many women on a daily basis, especially at conferences, who look like a hot mess. A real hot mess! I am not sure if their friends have encouraged them to dress the way they do or if they think wearing the latest style (which is *never* for everyone) is appealing.

I really think there needs to be a law that prevents folks from leaving the house without consulting someone who is up to date on fashion trends and styles.

This is where your real-world Gay Best Friend comes in handy; if you have one, call him up. Have him come over. Whatever you do, make sure you consult with him before leaving the house.

If you are caught out of your house looking wrong, busted, and disgusted, then he should be given a ticket by the fashion police. Your Gay Best Friend should be arrested and locked away. His license to sip Moscato should be revoked and his Tiffany crystal wand destroyed.

---

Let's talk about attire and appearance. Lawdy, lawdy, lawdy. I tell you.

You should *see* some of the women I see out in public at events. They have on dresses that are revealing *way* too much information. I should not be able to see the areola of your nipple. I should not see your butt cheeks. I definitely do not need to know what color panties you have on, or whether you are wearing any.

I wonder if some women watch BET and MTV to get fashion ideas and think it is suitable attire to wear on the streets or even to work. Then those women get upset when men talk about them and treat them the way they do.

If you dress like a common whore, then guess what? You will be treated like a common whore. And as your Gay Best Friend, I am telling those women to stop dressing like teenagers when even the teenagers themselves don't dress like that.

I am not saying you shouldn't show some skin, but having your behind and ta-tas out is neither cute nor attractive. Especially if you are a big girl. Learn to dress age- and occasion-appropriately. There is a time and place for everything.

If you want to dress like a video chick, save it for the bedroom or Halloween. I know it's sometimes hard to keep the freak in you quiet, but the less power you give her to run your life, the more you will be able to attract the right man for you.

Let me share a piece of advice I received from a very close friend of mine, "Pamela." She'd just gotten a job at a fashion magazine. Pamela was a recent college graduate and just starting out in her career. She did not have a lot of office/professional clothing. She also did not have a lot of money to go shopping immediately.

What Pamela did, however, was *invest* in her wardrobe. When she got paid every other week, she would go to Barneys, Lord & Taylor, and Bloomingdale's. Yes, we love these stores.

Pamela would purchase a classic and timeless top and bottom piece. She told me she was not interested in the hottest trends, but in the quality of her clothing—silks, cottons, *breathable* cottons. Not only was she thinking about the future of her wardrobe, but she was also thinking about her appearance and what image she wanted to project. Style and grace go a long way, baby.

Now, I am not saying you have to go to any of these stores.

Well, actually I am.

But if you live in an area where there is a Gucci, Prada, Dolce & Gabbana, Bebe, Nicole Miller, Versace, or Donna Karan, think about investing in some of their classic pieces.

So, you don't have a lot of money. Guess what? Most of these designers have outlet stores, online shopping, or sample sales in major cities. Even the major department stores have outlets, such as Nordstrom Rack and Saks Off Fifth. And don't we all love a good sale?

Imagine what you can find if you take the time to invest at least three days a week shopping. (Okay, okay, at least two days a week. Sheesh! You are making your Gay Best Friend cringe.)

Trust me, you will be grateful and happy when you see your wardrobe fill up with fine quality clothing instead of the latest and hottest trends that are out of season before you get a good wear out of them.

Here's another tip Pamela shared. It's something I also do. Put money into your shoes. I can't tell you enough that if you treat your feet cheaply, they will tell on you. I see women who are fly and fine from the ankle up. When you get to their shoes, oh my gosh, they are wearing worn out, run-over, and busted shoes. What is really going on?

When I was a child, my mother always told me you can tell a lot about a man by the shoes he wears. My grandfather would spend at least a hundred dollars on a single pair of shoes every other week. He was a sharp-dressed man. He never wore jeans. He only wore slacks, collared shirts, blazers, Stetson hats, and his Johnston & Murphy or Salvatore Ferragamo shoes. My grandmother was right beside him, dressed to the nines, matching him head to toe. She didn't skimp on her appearance, especially her footwear.

Let's look at the average amount some ladies spend on coffee from Starbucks and eating out for lunch every day.

Coffee = $10 (Starbucks twice a day)

Lunch = $10

That's $20 a day.

Multiply that by 5 times a week.

This adds up to $100 a week.

Now multiply that by 4 weeks.

You spend $400 a month, just on coffee and lunch.

That's a fabulous pair of Giuseppes, Christian Louboutin, Manolo Blahnik, Jimmy Choo, Gucci, or Prada pumps. Yes, yes, yes!

And Miss Thang, in those shoes you will be *strutting* down the street, giving Carrie Bradshaw a run for her money. Work it!

Come on now. Tell me it's not worth the sacrifice. You get to start a collection of pumps that will have your feet singing "Hallelujah" (as well as the man who will be kissing and sucking on those pretty toes, less the corns and bunions).

---

Now finally, beyond looks, let's talk about your *intellectual* style. Don't get me started on people (both gentlemen and ladies) who join a conversation and don't know what the *hell* they are talking about.

On the other side, there are those who know *every* damn thing. They are experts on health, culture, law, business, beauty, and fashion. (Yet they always seem to be the ones with all the issues and problems.)

If you are not knowledgeable on a subject, the elegant thing to do is keep your mouth closed. Do some research on the subject, and then research it some more before you form an opinion.

If you are not sure how a word is pronounced, don't say it. Look it up and learn the correct pronunciation first.

Now that I've gotten that off my chest, Ms. Honey, here is a serious suggestion. If you would like to enhance your knowledge on *any* subject, there are community centers, workshops, and cultural institutions that offer free classes. That's correct. You can go online, visit your local library, or check your church's bulletin board to see what programs are being offered, then go out and become knowledgeable on anything that interests you—real estate, photography, art, or music.

Did you know most museums offer free courses on art and collecting? That's right. You can go to the Studio Museum in Harlem or the Metropolitan Museum of Modern Art. Whatever city you live in, the museums offer workshops to help those who are artistically deprived.

Most libraries offer free writing workshops, and there are a plethora of books and lectures there that can help you become conversant in nearly any field or subject matter. Most companies also offer their employees opportunities to advance in their career by taking classes or doing fellowships at local community colleges or universities.

The point I am making here is there is no reason why you can't enhance your mind as well as your looks. Beauty and brains make a *fierce* combination. And when you have a fan-tab-u-lous real-life Gay Best Friend to tag along with you? Just imagine the possibilities.

I am getting goose bumps just thinking about it.

A Diva constantly works to upgrade her cultural tastes and intellect. Each year there are taste fests in every big city. Many restaurants participate, because they want to attract new customers. They have samplings of their menus available, and the food is delicious. These events will allow you the opportunity to let go of the local corner chicken spot, the take-out Chinese down the block, or chains like Red Lobster and Applebee's. Your palate will love you, along with your man (once you find him—that is, if you haven't already).

I can't tell you how many times I've heard from men who go out on dates and the woman can't even suggest a restaurant or activity. Then when the men make a suggestion and take her out someplace she's never been, you'd think he was asking her to join him on an African safari.

Take the time to check inside your daily local paper or the weekend section of your city's weekly magazine. You are bound to find lots of activities and places to explore that are outside of your neighborhood. There are many free events such as art festivals, cultural events, book readings, lectures, and concerts. Don't be afraid to explore and attend these activities.

If you are seeking to attract a spiritual man in your life, he will be interested in how intelligent you are, but he will also be interested in how awesome and wonderful you look in a dress, with makeup and your hair done. He will like to be fed mentally and physically. So knock his socks off with your feminine wiles and your intellect.

## Chapter 7

# Working 9 to 5:
# Is This a Way To Make a Living?

How many of you ladies are currently working a nine-to-five? Come on now, a show of hands.

Raise them high. Higher.

Higher.

Whew! Just as I thought. It's a lot of you.

How many of you would rather be doing something other than working the current job you have?

What is it? What do you desire deep down inside to earn a living? You know. Like, your dream career.

I remember when I was thirteen years old in my hometown of Detroit. I was at my aunt's home, where I discovered an album in a blue sleeve. (Yes, I said album. Not CD. Don't act like you don't know what an album is. It's a black round thing that is made of vinyl. Sheesh!) Anyway, I put the album on the record player and put the needle on the record and got the shock of my life. It was a rap group, the Sugar Hill Gang, rapping a song called "Rapper's Delight." I was mesmerized listening to the lyrics. At that moment, I was hooked. I played the record over and over again until I'd memorized every word.

I knew right then I wanted to be a part of this phenomenon exploding across America called hip-hop.

I researched and digested everything I could find about hip-hop. I discovered it was the happening scene in New York City. I started daydreaming and plotting how I was going to get to New York to be a part of the culture and lifestyle, like the burgeoning rappers who made it look so cool. I read *Black Beat* and *Right On!* I was in awe staring at the images of Run DMC, LL Cool J, Kool Moe Dee, Salt-n-Pepa, and Heavy D and The Boyz. They had on their Levi's jeans, Adidas sneakers, Kangol hats, and big gold chains. Yes, I wanted to be a part of it. I had to.

Ten years later, after graduating high school and college, I was living in New York City and working in the entertainment industry. My dream had become a reality.

Don't get me wrong, the road to my dream wasn't an easy one. I worked unpaid internships. I lived and slept on friends' floors and sofas. There were lots of hungry days when I had nothing to eat but a Snickers bar and a bag of potato chips. I heard from many people, the naysayers, who told me I shouldn't work in the entertainment industry and that I should get a real job. But I didn't listen to them. I stayed focused on my dream and went after it.

The point I am making is that whatever you desire in a career, you have to dream it, see it, and believe it. Whatever you dream of, you can make a living doing it. People will pay you for your services, especially if you are doing what you love, because you will do it with a smile on your face and joy in your heart.

I am certain that you never dreamed you would be sitting at a desk, hating your job and dreading going to work each day. That is not what you envisioned for yourself.

You saw yourself as an actress, dancer, singer, writer, doctor, lawyer, CEO, or whatever you dreamed. The job you are going to from nine to five is not it. Not what you went to high school and graduated for. Not what you went to college and shelled out thousands of dollars for. This is not it.

It can't be, right? *Is this what I did it all for?* You say to yourself. *This is not my dream.*

I am here to let you know that this is not a way to make your living. There is still time to make your dreams a reality. This isn't the end of the line, road, or rope. You've got options. You can still get back on track to your dream.

Yes, we all get sidetracked, but it's no reason to stay on the road less traveled. (Especially not wearing some fierce Manolo Blahniks or Christian Louboutin pumps. As your Gay Best Friend, I will not have you out there like that).

I am all for helping people get to where they want to be, especially having the career they deserve. The last thing I want to do is listen to someone complain about her current job or situation, especially when she can do something about it.

It wears me out to no end when I hear people constantly complaining about their jobs. How much they hate it. They hate waking up and going to that dreadful place where they cannot get along with their coworkers or boss. They arrive late and are the first ones out the door at five o'clock. They don't take on additional work and will not stay late. It is just a job and a paycheck and they treat it just as such.

I remember when I was at MTV Networks. I loved my job. I loved going to work, staying late, working on different projects and assisting others. I looked forward to doing it every day. It was what I had dreamed about as a kid. I had the dream job. I got to travel to various cities throughout the United States. I got to work with celebrities, many of whom are my friends to this day. I worked on great programs and award shows that people tuned in to watch from their living rooms. I was actually there experiencing it live and in person.

Yes, I loved my job.

But you want to know what? There were people who worked with me who *hated* working at MTV. They didn't want to be there. They complained and bitched about their jobs. They couldn't care less about any of the projects and the other opportunities afforded them working at MTV.

I didn't understand why they were there if they hated it so much. They had good cushy jobs, yet they didn't want to be there. Why were they there, taking up space, when so many people who really wanted to work at MTV would never get the opportunity? I could never figure that out.

Then one day it dawned on me. No matter what job people had, or career they were in, if they were not doing what they had dreamed, nothing would make them happy. Yup, people need fulfillment in their lives, and it has to be doing something they really love and desire.

So, whenever my friends call me or we are out on the town and they start complaining about their jobs, I immediately stop the conversation and say, "If you don't like your job and you hate it so much, then quit."

Girl, you can imagine the looks and stares I get from my friends? "Why would you say something like that?" They say to me. "I got bills to pay. I can't just quit. How would I pay my rent?"

"Then stop complaining about your job and be glad you got one," I say.

"It's easy for you to say that because you have a great job."

"Yes, I do. I love what I do. I didn't settle along the way to my dream, and you shouldn't either."

Girlfriend, listen up and listen up well. If you don't like your job—if you hate it, and you don't look forward to going to work every day—then you need to quit and move on. Let someone who really wants to be in your spot have it. You are taking someone else's dream from them by sitting in their chair when you could be living the dream you really have for yourself.

I don't want to hear it.

*I don't want to hear it.*

Yes, I repeated that line twice.

I know you are saying, "But Terrance, I got bills. I got rent to pay. I got a car note. How am I going to eat? I got things to do. I need my job." Well, if that's really the beginning and end of the story, then you need to stop complaining. Because if you keep saying what you don't like about your job and those you work with, the universe will conspire to make your thoughts of no longer working there become a reality. I have seen it happen time and time again.

Ever notice those folks who get laid off or fired from their jobs and are upset and crying? They don't know why it happened to them. But it's those same people who constantly complained about their jobs or said they didn't like where they worked and wanted something better.

The universe only responded and made their thoughts a reality. They got what they desired.

If you sit there saying negative things about your job and then you find yourself in the unemployment line, don't ask why it happened to you. You will know why.

So what do you need to do to get your dream career, or job?

Go after it. Research what you need to do to make it happen, and go for it. Sitting at your desk every day wondering, wishing, and hoping is not going to make it happen. Sitting in your living room watching others on television live their dreams will not get you discovered.

I am not saying it's not going to be a cakewalk or an easy road. Anything worth getting is worth working hard for. There will be times you will want to give up, but keep your eyes on the prize.

There will be those who will say to you, "Why are you doing that? Why did you quit your job making money? You had it good."

No one knows what your dreams or desires are but you. No one can understand the feeling in your heart and soul when you are going after your dream. It's an amazing and compelling feeling. You wake up thinking about it. You go to bed thinking about it. You dream of it all day.

Girl, I am telling you, it will eat at your soul, but it's a hunger that fulfills you and makes you feel full. It's so good!

I have met so many people on my tours and speaking engagements who want to work in the entertainment industry but don't live where it is happening. If you desire to be a singer or actor, then you need to find a way to move to New York City or Los Angeles. Agents, casting directors, managers, producers, and directors don't know where you live. They are not going to show up on your doorstep looking for you. Record company executives will not discover you singing in your house in Alabama, Mississippi, or Missouri. As much as you may hope they will come to you, a record executive will not knock on your door, ready to give you a recording contract.

Even if that is not your career goal, but you desire to do something else, and the career of your dreams is in another city, or state, then *move*. Go for it. What do you have to lose?

Oh, let me guess. You don't know anyone in that city. You don't have any friends in that state. You will be leaving your family.

Uhm, trust me, darling. You will make new friends, and you can always visit your family. Don't let that be a diversion.

The obstacles and hurdles you face going after your dreams are created by you. Yes, they are. *You* say what you can't and will not do. *You* decide why you are unable to have what you really desire.

Well, it stops now.

No more complaining.

No more whining.

I don't want to hear it anymore.

It's time to let go of those negative thoughts, and the shoulda-coulda-wouldas. Whatever you desire to have, you can have it. If you are ambitious and know that you deserve success, then it cannot elude you. The only thing standing between you and your dream is you!

But you couldn't have told "Leslie" this.

Girl, I tell you, there are some people who ask you for advice (or rather, they tell you all their problems and wait for your answer), but they don't really want an answer. They just rant on and on and on about how wrong things are, that people are idiots, that their job is menial and it's a waste of their time.

Yes, that is Leslie.

I met Leslie through a mutual friend and we immediately hit it off. She didn't have a Gay Best Friend in her life, and because I am blunt and to-the-point, she fell in love with me. And me, I like a fly woman who is doing her thing and making it look effortless.

Leslie was an executive in the entertainment industry and had a great job. She met and hung out with celebrities. She was on every industry list for movie premieres, concerts, openings, red carpets, dinners, and other major events in the city. People wanted her in attendance.

Leslie's job required for her to be there, but she would've rather been someplace else. She often declined the invitations, or she would RSVP and not show up. Most times she would call me to attend with her, but once we were there, she would complain and want to leave after only twenty minutes.

"Terrance, I am *so* over these events and fake people," Leslie said to me. "My job is stressful enough, and then I have to attend these events almost every night when I would rather be at home relaxing."

"But isn't it your job to be at these events to network and cover them for your company?" I asked.

"Yes, but it's only me. I don't have any assistants who can help cover all these events. They need to get someone else to do it. I can't do everything."

I didn't say anything after that. I knew if we'd continued the conversation, she'd have gone into the "I-hate-my-job" rant. So I let well enough alone because I don't like to hear people complain.

As time went on, Leslie became extremely vocal with me about the dislikes of her job. "I hate my job. I need something else. I've started looking, but I'm so busy I can't really focus on my job search."

"What is it you don't like about your job?" I hesitantly asked.

And it began. The rant. The long tirade about her dislikes and utter disgust with her job. Our conversations (well, her conversations) about her job were going in one ear and out the other by this point. I'd gotten tired of hearing her complain about her job. When she called, her name would flash across my cell phone screen and sometimes I wouldn't even answer because I knew the conversation would just end up being another of her constant complaints. Even when she sent text messages, I wouldn't respond.

Leslie continued to extend invitations to industry events, but I declined. Her negative energy was too much for me. At times I wanted to yell, "Shut the hell up and stop complaining about your job before you don't have one!" But I didn't. I just avoided her.

During one of the rare calls I took from her, I asked Leslie, again, what she didn't like about her job, and I instantly regretted the words ever leaving my lips. She talked for an hour, telling me how incompetent people at her job were. She didn't like certain employees. She needed more money, and an assistant. The long hours she spent on her job was taking away from her personal life. She was getting physically sick. She couldn't manage to wake up in time for work and she was always late.

"You know what?" I said. "You better hurry up and find another job, or just quit."

"Boy, I can't quit in this market. It's a recession. I got bills to pay. I got rent."

I pulled the phone from my ear and stared at it. Here was my moment to be honest and tell her the truth, or just get off the phone.

I chose the latter.

If I'd stayed on the phone and given her my opinion about what to do, she wouldn't have heard me anyway. Over the months, I'd already talked until I was blue in the face, giving her advice. She hadn't followed any of my suggestions yet, so I wasn't going to waste my time or words any longer.

I was just going to sit back and watch things unfold.

Leslie began to experience physical sicknesses that no doctor in the entire city of New York could diagnose. She was unable to sleep at night due to a persistent cough. She was vomiting in her sleep and she experienced shortness of breath. Every week she had an appointment with a new doctor. None could tell her what was going on with her. Finally one doctor told her she was making herself sick.

When Leslie told me what the doctor said, I shook my head and said, "You think?"

Then a month later, it was all in the press. Her company had downsized and she was one of the people who had been let go. I'd seen it coming. I wasn't shocked when I got her call. I wasn't nearly as surprised as she was.

Oh, girl, you should have heard her bitching and cursing. How the company had done her wrong, and the few people who weren't laid off were the ones who should've been let go. I just let her vent because, again, whatever I could have said, she wouldn't have heard me. She was caught up in everyone else being wrong and how the world around her was somehow screwed up. But not her. Nope. She had it all together.

All I kept thinking while she was yapping on the phone was, *You got exactly what you asked for. All the days you were late to work. The constant complaints about being overworked, your co-workers' incompetence, and how much you hated your job. How you made yourself sick and went from doctor to doctor each week only to be told it was you who was making yourself sick. Your losing your job was your own doing.*

Ladies, pay close attention to what you are saying, who you are saying it to, and more important, why are you saying it.

If you don't like where you are as it relates to your job, don't sit around complaining about it. *Do* something about it. If that means going back to school to learn a skill, then do it. If it means staying up at night burning the midnight oil, then do it. Success comes at a price, and you must be willing to make sacrifices to accomplish your goals and have your dreams come true. The truth is, there is *nothing* you can't do. You are fierce, destined, and fabulous. But if you think you can't have it, then you won't.

Did you know that the best-selling author Terry McMillan was a single mother and had a full-time job when she wrote her first book? She would awaken extra early in the morning to work on her novel before getting her child ready, and then head to work. She achieved her dream and is now making a living at it.

You know Grammy award-winning R&B singer Anita Baker? She was a receptionist in Detroit before she took the leap into singing. She achieved her dream and is making a living at it.

Those are only two examples, but there are so many more about powerful women who refused to let their dreams die or subside.

As your Gay Best Friend, I am telling you that Spirit has a plan for you. When Spirit speaks, I suggest you listen, move, and act, and let the steps on your journey lead you to your purpose and destiny.

# Chapter 8

# Ambitious: Not Am Bitches

You know what is unattractive in a woman? A woman who *brags* that she is a bitch. She is inconsiderate, rude, snappy, angry, and downright nasty. So unladylike.

Why would a woman want to be a bitch? What is so attractive about that? Does she think a man will say, "I want to be with her! I need a bitch in my life."

Hell, naw!

Even in the workplace, I have witnessed some women who feel they have to be bitchy and nasty to everyone, because if they don't, nobody will take them seriously. They scratch and claw their way to the top of the corporate ladder, leaving behind a destructive trail of ruined friendships, hateful co-workers, and people whose only desire is to see them fail, waiting for the day those bitchy women come tumbling down from their high chair of success, falling flat on their faces. Then they will dance and stomp all over them, as if they got the Holy Spirit, chanting and cheering the great fall.

Peaches, let me tell you something. There is a big distinction between being ambitious and being a bitch. I am going to break it down for you.

Now, let me get my cocktail before you start saying I don't understand what it's like for a woman to have to fight her way to the top in a company, or build her name and be respected. I think this time I'll mix a Caribbean Kiss (I can only imagine how wet and juicy it is going to be).

Girl, we *all* want to be respected in the workplace. Many of us want to be perched in the black executive leather chair in the big corner office with the huge windows so everyone in the adjacent buildings can get a glimpse of us wearing our fabulous designer business suits and carrying our leather attaché bags. With our names inscribed in big gold letters on the door with our titles.

But as your trusty and loyal Gay Best Friend, I have to let you in on a big secret. Most truly successful women have done it without being a bitch.

They were determined and had ambition. But they were not bitches.

Ambition is being and living your dream. No one and nothing can take your dream away from you. What is meant for you, is meant for you. If you stay focused, remain clear about what your goals are, and build positive relationships with other people, you will get what is rightfully yours.

One of the biggest components of success is encouraging and helping other people. When you work with others and build them up as you climb your way to the top, they will *always* remember your generosity and help you make your dreams come true. People like to see others succeed, especially if they are included in the process and have a great relationship with the person they believe in.

I have seen it happen time and time again in the entertainment industry, where I worked for more than fifteen years. Let me tell you, the entertainment industry can be a cutthroat business. The women (and men) are something *fierce* in that business. Backstabbing one another, lying, deceiving, and even sabotaging one another. Everyone wants to shine, and they will do whatever it takes to hold the limelight in a project that becomes a success. It's more serious than any daytime soap opera drama. Hell, Erica Kane doesn't have *anything* on the shady characters in the entertainment world.

On a positive note, however, I have seen lots of women who start as the receptionist or secretary of the company to go on and become vice president, even president of the company. Why?

Because they built and nurtured relationships with *everyone*. They developed personal relationships with co-workers because they understood what it's like to have a family and work long hours, so they pitched in to help with last-minute projects. They sent flowers and cards to sick coworkers and remembered their birthdays. They praised other employees and gave credit where credit was due. They learned the inner workings of the company and when something went wrong, guess what? Everyone came to them because they knew who to call, or how to get it fixed.

Yes, they were the saviors, the unsung she-roes of the company. Now they are at the top, with lots of people who support and encourage them. These women have employees who are happy and willing to help them stay at the top. The women at the top want their employees to succeed and be great. They want them to win, because those women helped *them* to win.

Being the bitch in the company only sets you up for others to want to bring you down, quickly. They will smile to your face and talk about you behind your back. They don't want to be on your team when it's time for a big project. They will try to sabotage you, even if it's to the detriment of the project. They *hate* to see you coming. They don't want to be around you, and everyone is waiting for the day of your termination.

Bitchiness is yelling and screaming at people who are subordinate to you. You treat them not as people, but as your servants. You don't know how to say "thank you" when others help you with a project. You climb over and on top of people to get what you want, when you want it, and how you want it.

Maybe the person I am describing isn't you, but don't sit there like you don't know who that woman is. As soon as you read the description, someone you knew popped into your head. And you were probably one of those who experienced her wrath. You couldn't stand her. You and your co-workers talked about her behind her back. You cursed her under your breath. You wrote about her on Facebook and other social networking websites. You prayed for the day she would be fired. She got on your last nerve.

No, you don't want to be like her. You are a lady. A Diva! And I am going to get you to the top with a little assistance by adjusting your attitude, personality, and charm.

Oh, yes, everyone loves to be charmed. And naturally, as a woman, you can charm the pants off a man in the middle of Times Square in New York City and walk away with him in tow, following and doing whatever you want him to do.

Okay, so, first things first.

You have to smile.

Yes, open your mouth and show those pearly white teeth. (Well, hopefully you've got some pearly white teeth. If not, get some tooth whitening gel, or hurry up and get to the dentist).

Smiling warms the soul. It's inviting. It's pure adulation. When people see you smiling, they smile.

Walking around with a scowl on your face makes you appear unapproachable. People don't want to be around you. In fact, they run away from you. However, when you smile, it lifts your *own* spirits and makes your interactions with others very pleasant. People *want* to be around you. They want to help you when you ask for assistance, because you do it with a smile. You appear joyous and happy. Such a person is someone others want to associate with.

Next, you have to say, "Thank you." Yes, those two words will get you far. When you thank others for their hard work, commitment, and assistance, they don't mind going out of their way to do things for you. They feel appreciated and not used.

Give credit and praise. Lawd, I can't *tell* you how so many people will sit in a board meeting, or in their boss's office, and not give credit or praise to their fellow employees. You know, the ones who slaved and worked long hours on the project with them, and now these people have the gall to sit there taking all the credit. That is so selfish and inconsiderate.

And trust me, the boss is paying attention.

The self-declared "bitch" thinks the boss is not looking or noticing what's happening in her department, but the boss *is*.

Then when the bitch doesn't get the promotion, she wonders why. I just want to say to her, "Honey, you didn't give credit where credit was due. You didn't do all that work yourself. How dare you take the credit for someone else's hard work?"

Here's another way to be a bitch. Throw your education and title around, belittling those you feel are beneath you. Walk around like your mess doesn't stink with your nasty attitude, bragging about your education that cost over a hundred and fifty thousand dollars (of which you still owe a hundred and fifteen). Acting all high and mighty.

I want to tell these women, "Stop it! Stop thinking you're better than others, because you're not."

If all you do is talk about your education and the fact that you are the director of this or vice president of that, well then, sweetheart, don't be surprised if people roll their eyes at you. They may even pretend, to make you think you're as important as you think you are. But when it comes down to it, guess who will get the job? Not the bitch, and not her credentials that she flaunts and throws around.

The job will go to the woman who has the experience and likability, and who can get the job done efficiently because she works as a team player. People like people who get along well with others. You've got to play nice. Then others will play nice with you.

Be a bitch and you will create bitchy people who will constantly complain and will not want to work with you.

I had a friend, "Kayla," who was a corporate Diva. I mean she was Miss It, and an Ivy-league graduate. Honey, Ms. Kayla dressed to the nines in her name-brand designer suits with shoes to kill for. When she walked, Kayla had a strut in her step that said, "I'm fly and bossy. Get out my way!"

I think R&B singer Kelis based her hit song "Bossy" on women like Kayla.

Kayla was on the climb in a Fortune 500 company. Talk about fast-track. She was on it. In a year she'd gone from assistant in her department to assistant manager. In another six months, she was the manager. A year later, Kayla was named director of her department.

Kayla had a hunger. A thirst to be vice president. And I had no doubt she could get there.

We had plenty of conversations about her strong and strict work ethic. "Terrance, I don't play with my employees," Kayla said. "I crack a whip on them. When I walk into the room, they jump."

"That is not a good thing," I said. "Do you want your employees to fear you or respect you?"

"Both!" She practically screamed. "You don't understand. I *have* to put my foot down or else they won't respect me. I have three things going against me. I'm young, black, and a woman. That intimidates people."

I looked her over and shook my head.

"What?" She asked. "I *know* you've got something to say."

She was right. I had plenty to say.

Kayla was my friend, and although I really respected her and appreciated her desire to get to the top, I certainly did not agree with the way she was going about it.

"Miss Diva, I am going to say this and say it once. Just because people fear you doesn't mean they respect you. Being a bitch is not cute. Not in the workplace, where people have to report to you and you are chewing out their heads. How would you feel if someone were constantly standing over you and cracking the whip to perform? You wouldn't like it, would you?"

Miss Kayla put her hand on her hip and jerked her head back with her long luxurious lace-front weave and said, "I am not trying to be their friend. This isn't high school or college. I am their boss. I've got to let them know who runs things."

"Well, then, I guess you told me." I smirked.

Because I knew what was going to happen next.

It was only a matter of time.

A few months later, Kayla called me, ecstatic. "Oh my gosh, Terrance! I just got another promotion. I am the new senior director."

"Good for you," I said. I really *was* happy for Kayla. Then I asked, "How is being a bitch working out for you? Are you still cracking that whip?"

"I'm still on top of them," she laughed. "And I am not a bad bitch. I am a good bitch. I don't take any mess. Besides, I am being watched. I am not going to let my staff bring me down. I will get rid of anyone who gets in my way."

"I'm here for you when you need me," I said.

"What is that supposed to mean?" Kayla asked.

"I'm just saying when things get tough, I am here for you."

"Things are going well, and as long as I keep my department in check, nothing can go wrong."

I smirked again.

This time I looked at the date on the calendar, because I knew within six months to a year, Kayla wouldn't be singing that same tune.

Sure enough, six months later Kayla was on my phone, boo-hooing. The screech in her voice when I answered said it all.

"Terrance, I got fired!" She yelled through tears.

I thought about saying, "Aha, I told you being a bitch would be your demise." But I figured I'd find out what happened before I said anything.

"What happened?"

"They said my performance and attitude were not in alignment with the company's. And do you know, none of my employees said anything to me as I was packing my things. They didn't even come in and ask what happened. They acted as if they were happy to see me go."

*You think?!* I screamed in my head.

Before I consoled her, because I am her Gay Best Friend, I had to tell it to her straight. "Kayla, being a bitch is not being ambitious. The way you treated your employees, hell, I am surprised the company kept you around this long. When you walk over people and mistreat them, trust and *believe* those same people are going to be happy to see you fall, and they probably had a hand in it."

"You think they set me up?" She asked.

"Are you listening to anything I am saying?" I said, frustrated. "Girl, stop being a bitch!"

But Kayla wasn't interested in anything I had to say.

For she, and so many women in the workplace, feel they have to be hard, strong, and bitchy to get what they want and to make it to the top.

I let Kayla sulk for a few days before we had another conversation about her attitude, work ethic, and personality.

I figured if I gave her some time to think about what I'd said, it may actually have set in.

Sure enough, with a few days' distance, Kayla understood what I meant when I told her the difference between being a bitch and being ambitious.

"I am so glad to have a friend like you," Kayla said. "Thanks for telling me the truth about myself."

And that is why I hope you ladies reading this will understand that only a good friend, well, a Gay Best Friend, will tell you the truth about yourself.

It's okay to be determined, focused, and have aspirations. You need all that to succeed. It is part of the DNA for success.

People love to hear stories about those who overcome and push forward despite the odds against them. Especially women who make it in the workplace, where many offices are dominated by men and you are a member of a minority climbing the ladder to the top. Ambition is what many companies look for in their employees. Someone who is goal-oriented, a team player, driven, and has great ideas. But you've got to remember that your success is only really considered success when you help others along the way, and let them be a part of yours.

Being a bitch, well, let's save that for the movies, and soap opera dramas.

Because only fictional characters like Erica Kane, Alexis Carrington, and Dominique Deveraux do it oh so well.

## Chapter 9

# Family Dearest: You Can Pick Your Friends, But Not Your Family

Family. You've got to love them. I mean that literally. You've *got* to love them.

They certainly are not like friends, whom we can pick and choose. No, Miss Thang. Your family is yours by *inheritance*. They are part of your DNA, background, and future. They will *always* be a part of you—even when you may want them out of your life.

And some of them we truly wish were not part of our family tree.

Whew! Child, you know the ones. They won't let you be the Diva you are, especially while you're living the high life fabulously. Every step you take forward, they are right there to pull you back two steps. Grabbing your coattails and tugging on your fierce Valentino gown. LET ME GO!

But still, they pull and grab at you. You can't bring your new boyfriend around because you know they are going to embarrass you. There is the uncle who gets drunk at all the family gatherings, showing out and cursing at everyone. There is your aunt who is caught in a time warp—she still thinks she is a teenager and dresses like one, with too-little, too-tight clothes. There's the *other* aunt who thinks she is better than everybody else because she went to college and has a good job. Now her family lives in the suburbs and her children attend private schools, and she rarely comes to family events because she is "always busy."

There is the cousin who is always in and out of jail. You can't leave anything around him because it will come up missing. There is the other cousin who always wants to borrow some money from you.

And let's not forget about your sister, who loves sharing your business with everyone else, even when you tell her to keep it to herself. The entire family is talking about you behind your back and you wonder why they are staring at you when you walk into a room. Oh, yes—and your sister also loves to borrow things from you and never return them. Like your skirt, dress, jeans, shoes, boots, purse, and wigs.

There is your brother, who has ongoing problems with his woman and always runs to you for advice, but doesn't ever take or use any of it.

And let's not forget your parents. They try to run your life. They still treat you as if you are a child and refuse to let you grow up and be an adult. Yes, your parents get on your nerves sometimes, but you love your mother and father because they are always there for you, whether or not you like their advice.

One thing about your family. If you're lucky, they will always have your back. Despite the good times or the bad, they will step up to the plate and come to your aid.

Well, depending on what the aid may be.

If it has something to do with money, sometimes money and family don't necessarily gel so easily.

I have seen so many people fall out with family members, and it's always over money. The borrowing of it, the lending of it, and the inability to get it back.

I am a firm believer that money and family don't mix. If someone in my family comes to me asking to borrow some money, I tell them, "I am not going to let you borrow any money from me. I am going to *give it to you*. I am giving it to you because I know if you borrow it, you may not be able to pay me back. I want to maintain our good standing and not have a falling out over money."

Girl, let me tell you, that gesture alone alleviates so much tension and expectation. Because instead of them giving me some sob story and the promise, "I am going to pay you back at the end of the week when I get paid," or "You are going to get your money back at the end of the month," I don't *ever* have to hunt them down looking for my money. Instead of paying me back, they do something else with the money. I don't have to worry about them avoiding my calls and dodging me at family events because they know they haven't paid me back. I give them the money up front, without any obligations.

I know many of you may not be in a situation to lend money, but if you can, and family members come to you asking to borrow money, then *give it* to them. Don't lend it. Let them have it. If you give them the money, you don't have to worry about a big family fight over it. Because, sweet thang, you know when that happens, the entire family gets involved with folks giving their advice and taking sides. That is a hot mess.

Family should be about love. Unconditional love. No matter who they are, what they do, and what you may not like about them.

"But how can I love my family when they have hurt me, or they've done something I don't like?" You may be asking.

It isn't easy, but when you can learn to accept people for who they are, and not for whether they live up to your expectations of them, then you truly can appreciate and love your family members. Once you let go of expectations, you can love your drunk uncle, because you know every time he shows up, he is going to get drunk. That is just who he is.

You can love your forty- or fifty-something aunt who thinks she is in her early twenties, because that's her life. What she wears and how she dresses has nothing to do with you. Let her live her life, because that is who she is.

The same goes for your brother who asks for advice all the time about his relationships and what he should do. Love him regardless, because that is who he is. He will always be your brother who seeks advice, but will end up doing his own thing. You know that about him, and you don't have to worry and get upset when he does what you already know he is going to do.

Even when your sister wants to borrow something from you. Give it to her. Let her have it and know you are not going to get it back. Or you can say, "No. You can't borrow it. No. I will not lend it to you." You already know how your sister is. You know she doesn't know how to return things. She is not going to change. That is just the way she is.

You understand, girl?

Love them despite it all, because that is *just who they are.* No amount of anger, upset, or bitterness toward them is going to make them change. Once you can let go of the expectations you have for your family members, you can love and appreciate them.

I'm already there.

It feels good to go to an event and just have fun without expectations getting in the way of my love for my family. I know them. I know what they are going to do and say. I actually look forward to being around my family, because I am in a place where I can love them unconditionally, and I let them love *me* in their own way.

I wasn't always in this place, but I got here with lots of prayer. Lord knows it takes a lot of prayer to be around my family.

I've moved beyond the previous hurt, anger, and bitterness I harbored for them.

I was bitter and angry for a long time, though. One reason was over my family's inability to coordinate a gathering without someone asking, "Why am I giving you my money?" Or "What is so-and-so bringing? She has a bigger family so she needs to bring more." And "Why can't so-and-so do it at her house? Why we always have to do it at my house?" They wore me out with all the questions over a simple get-together.

I was also very angry with my family over my mother and two brothers dying from AIDS. I talk about it extensively in my book, *Hiding in Hip Hop.*

Girl, I've told you about the situation with my mother and how my grandmother raised us because of my mother's inability to care for her children. I watched various men come to my grandmother's house, dropping off and picking up my mother in different cars. I always wondered why my mother disappeared for days, and months, without inquiring about her children. I didn't understand why my mother never demonstrated any type of love toward me and my siblings. I grew to despise my mother. I was hurt, disappointed, and oftentimes sad because I didn't have my mother around.

For a long time I carried anger and hatred toward my mother. When I grew older, I didn't like being around her. I learned of her addiction to drugs. I learned of her prostitution. It really bothered me, and I refused to speak to my mother for a long time. It wasn't until she developed AIDS, and I noticed the physical changes in her, that I began to let go of some of my resentment toward my mother.

It was hard to see my once beautiful, statuesque mother wither away. The disease was ravaging her body and there was nothing anyone could do. I silently cried, wanting to hold my mother and let her know everything was going to be all right. I wanted to comfort her because as the days went on, she rarely smiled or laughed.

Then finally, one day, I sat and spoke with my mother. We talked about *everything*. It was so refreshing to be able to have a conversation with my mother and let go of my hatred. I realized as we were speaking that my mother had done the best she could under the circumstances. I let go of my resentment and I forgave her and myself.

I forgave her because she only did what she knew what to do. Drugs had a grip on her life and made her unable to care for her children. I forgave myself because I had held on to so much anger and bitterness that it had prevented me from moving forward in my own life and having a relationship with my mother.

Once I forgave, I understood that my mother loved her children enough to allow us to be raised by our grandmother, a strong and resilient woman. My mother knew we would be in great hands with my grandmother.

I also let my mother be my mother. I didn't make her wrong. I didn't let her stop her motherly duties and responsibility. I let her be who she was and I finally opened my eyes and saw a woman who loved me and was very proud of me. My mother told me this over and over again during our talks.

I often hear people say they are angry and upset with their parents. They are not speaking with them, or they had a falling out over something minute. They get angry and yell at their mothers on the phone, not wanting to have a conversation because they are too busy.

Ms. Diva, if that is you, that is *not* fabulous. It's unnecessary and rude. I am going to tell you, you shouldn't be that way with your mother. At least you have a mother you can talk with and see whenever you want. You should treasure these moments and times, because you don't know when she will leave this earth. You don't know when *you* will leave this earth. You don't know what it's like to not have your mother in your life. So let go of the anger, hurt, and bitterness.

If you are currently in a dispute or disagreement with a family member, especially a parent, I am telling you right now, sweetness, let it go. Forgive your family member and yourself. Why are you sitting around pouting and walking around with an attitude? Is it really worth it? Does being upset with your parents make you right? Can you let go of being right for the sake of love? So they said something you didn't like. So what! They did something that pissed you off. Call them up and resolve the issue.

There are very few problems or situations that should prevent you from making amends with the people who are important in your life. If you learn to let them be who they are, and appreciate the moments they have shared with you and the advice, love, and concern, you will usually find yourself laughing and desiring to be around them. That is the sign of a woman who is fabulous and has a fabulous life. You don't let things or people bring you down. When you are fabulous, you build people up. You encourage them to express and be themselves.

I am a strong advocate for building family relationships and creating events that keep families together. They are the glue and bond between a group of people that allows you to show unconditional love. The relationships you have with your family members are the first real relationships you have in your life. They teach you everything you need to know about people and intimate relationships. Yes, the cast of characters in your family is just preparation for the relationships you develop in the world.

Family teaches you about trust, honesty, friendship, and love. You learn about the nature of conflict and commitment, and how to maintain relationships. You also learn how to love people despite their faults (because Lord knows you don't have any...). If you are willing to appreciate and build positive relationships with your own family, the people who are closest to you, then the people in the rest of the world should be a piece of cake.

And between you and me, if we can put up with our own families, and the crazy events, parties, picnics, and reunions that are filled with moments that truly make us wonder if we are the only sane ones in the family, then we are *definitely* destined for greatness.

It takes an amazingly fierce person to be able to smile, laugh, kick off her shoes and get on the dance floor with her family and enjoy the moment. So, come on, girl, let's cha-cha slide next to Grandma and Grandpa. And you better bring me along to the next party. I want to get in the hustle line next to your young aunt and drunk uncle.

Just kidding.

# Chapter 10

# Forgive: 'Cause You Know Not What You Do

Imet women from all over while I was on my book tour for *Hiding in Hip Hop*. From New York, through Detroit, Atlanta, DC, Maryland, and Virginia, to Chicago. One thing I can say for certain—many women are in pain. I'm talking about that Billie Holiday, Etta James, Mary J. Blige type of pain. It's the sangin' of the blues, and it's coming straight from the gut. Their heart is on the line, and they're tired of being tired.

Too many of the women I met are just like that. Maybe—just maybe—so are you. You are in pain, angry, and upset. Why?Because somewhere in your life someone hurt you. Someone took your love for granted. Now you refuse to allow it to happen again. The culprit in many of the cases was a man. You fell deep and hard in love and gave of your time, resources, money, and Spirit in the relationship.

In the beginning, the man you met was attentive. He took you out to dinner, had flowers delivered, and sent beautiful romantic cards. So you told yourself you'd met "The One." He was your prince. Your knight in shining armor. He was kind, sweet, well-mannered, and intelligent. But there was something missing. You couldn't quite put your finger on it, but you knew there was something not all there.

Then, at some point, the truth was revealed. You discovered he had cheated or lied. Maybe he was emotionally unavailable. He'd stopped growing spiritually and mentally. He no longer was challenging or thought-provoking. He became the enemy—*your* enemy.

Once the relationship you had once hoped would last forever ended, you became bitter and angry. You could not believe you'd allowed yourself to get so deeply involved with that *evil* man. The low-down dirty dog. How dare he waste your time?

Then you wanted revenge. Sweet revenge. You wanted to break something. Anything. It didn't matter what. It could have been his neck, for all you cared (but you couldn't get to him).

Some of you spent several years in the relationship and now feel you will never find the man for you. Others are on the verge of leaving a relationship and are afraid you will not find another man.

I know you're thinking, *What's a woman to do? I'm tired of giving of myself and not getting anything in return. Where are all the good men, and why can't I meet one? I am tired of being hurt. I am tired of being abused. I am just plain ole' tired!*

Hold on, girl. Just hold on.

We are going to do some healing.

We are going to work on healing *you* first. Don't worry about them, him, or anybody else. Let's just focus on you.

Let's gather around with our Martini or wine glasses. (Or maybe this time we should order cocktails. Screaming Orgasms—oh, if only we could have them often—or Caribbean Kisses) Whatever your drink of choice, let's make sure you've got a good bottle of your favorite alcohol available.

Now, put on your best dress. That *knock-out* dress that causes men's head to turn and women to suck their teeth at you.

Put on a dash of your most expensive perfume—Dior, Chanel, or Carolina Herrera.

Slip into a pair of Christian Loubutins, Jimmy Choos, or Manolo Blahniks. I now raise my glass to you and deem you a Diva. Work it, girl!

Now, take a good look at yourself in the mirror. Look at how beautiful and amazing you are. This is how you should feel on the inside as well. If you exude confidence and self-worth on the inside, your outside will also shine.

However, a lot of sisters out there are still in pain and have experienced deep heartache. Fixing this is going to take my special magic potion of fierceness, love, and a dash of gay wisdom.

I would like to begin by encouraging you to forgive yourself. Not because you did anything wrong, but because you may feel you have no other choices. When most of you feel you have reached the end of your rope, you give up. You stop believing in yourself. When your relationship with a man falls apart, you attempt to do *everything* to pull it back together. I have seen some women do some crazy, absurd things. Calling him several times a day, texting him like a mad woman, filling up his BlackBerry, stalking him on every social networking website, and even enrolling friends to do drive-bys of his home to find out where he is and what he's doing. Pudding pop, STOP IT! Just stop it right now.

Let's look at the situation.

Have you ever stopped to think that maybe the relationship has run its course? Maybe it's time to let it go and move on. Maybe it's time to do for *you*. Love *you*, embrace *you*, fulfill *your* dreams. In case you haven't done so yet, it's time to forgive yourself.

You may have not been empowered with the spiritual knowledge to protect yourself—to protect your own Spirit and remain vigilant of your own spiritual development and nourishment. It's easy to become wrapped up in a man and lose sight of how valuable and important *you* are. You sometimes become negligent in nourishing yourself spiritually, because for some reason when a man and sex is involved, all your wisdom and common sense gets thrown out the window. Especially if the sex is really, really good. (My gosh, if he can put it on you! You lose all your senses, and everything you normally wouldn't do, you find yourself doing—getting him things on your credit card, buying him unnecessary items to prove your love, allowing him to move in with you despite him being in between jobs. Please, don't get me started.)

Instead of leaving an unhealthy relationship, some of you are encouraged by friends and family members time and time again to stay and make it work. Despite all the efforts and energy you have given men, they tell you not to walk away. And of course, this advice comes from other miserable and unhappy people (who don't have a Gay Best Friend in their life to advise them otherwise—thank goodness you have me).

Here is the truth: Girl, it is *okay* to walk away. It is okay to be angry and upset, but don't beat yourself up over it. Pull yourself together, straighten out your shoulders, raise your head, and strut your stuff. Heel, toe, heel, toe. Give Naomi Campbell a run for her money on the catwalk. Remember, you are number one.

So, forgive yourself, because you did all you could. You bent over backward, agreed when you wanted to disagree, nurtured him, and neglected yourself. Now it's time for *you*. Time to be all about *your own* needs.

And the first step to the healing process and moving forward is forgiving yourself.

Forgive because you allowed yourself to stay as long as you did. No one forced you to remain in an unhealthy relationship. Forgive because you did what you thought you should do. Most of you stayed because of what others advised you to do. Women tell each other, "Hang in there girl, it's hard out there for single women," or "Don't leave that man, at least he comes home at night." Let me tell you something. There are plenty of available, good-looking, strapping, intelligent, career-minded, and family-oriented men out there. Don't settle. Don't stay in a relationship to please your friends. If it's not working, it's not working. It's time to leave.

In *Reclaim Your Power!* I wrote about how forgiveness allows you the opportunity to let go of the pain you are dragging and carrying around with you. It's like Erykah Badu's song, "Bag Lady." She uses the analogy to explain how carrying stress, pain, and a lack of forgiveness keeps you in bondage and weighed down. In the song, Erykah sings:

> *Bag lady you gone hurt your back*
> *Dragging all them bags like that...*
> *Girl, I know sometimes it's hard*
> *And we can't let go*

*Oh when someone hurts you oh so bad inside*
*You can't deny it you can't stop crying*

Some women are trying to carry all their bags at one time. Lugging around Louis Vuitton, Coach, Dooney & Bourke, Birkin, and Prada bags filled with all their pain, hurt, anger, and disappointments. Trust me, those are some fab bags to have, but then you've got all those bags strapped on your shoulders and back, struggling through life because you don't know how to let go and put them down.

You think it's necessary to carry around all that baggage all at once? Put those bags down, now! It makes no sense you're walking around with all that mess. Let go of your past ills and hurts. It only keeps you weighed down and heavily burdened. Besides, if you don't, you will carry all that baggage into every relationship you enter.

When you forgive someone, it frees you of stress, pain, and hurt. Forgiving allows you to let Spirit move and work in your life to help heal your soul. Spirit can help you create a space in your life to love not only yourself, but others as well. *And when you stand praying, if you hold anything against anyone, forgive him, so that your Father in heaven may forgive you your sins* (Mark 11:25).

If you don't do the mature thing and forgive yourself, you will allow your anger and frustration to build up and fester. Yup, it sure will. You will be walking around in a perpetual angry mood, like you're PMSing forever. That is not cute. Besides, it can cause all sorts of ailments like stress, high blood pressure, and a permanent frown. And let me tell you one thing sister, you are too beautiful to let a man stress you.

Girl, let it go.

Like Rachel, whom I told you about in the first chapter. She needed to stop beating up on herself because she felt as if she had failed. She did not want to face her friends and family members after her "perfect" relationship crumbled. Although she knew her man was no good for her, she wanted to save face. Instead of listening to her own voice, her inner Spirit, Rachel had to find out the hard way.

She chose the experience and had to endure the heartbreak. It all could have been avoided if she would have listened to the spiritual guidance assisting her.

Rachel had to appear like she had it all together, because she was smart and beautiful. That's what most people do, anyway. Despite the pain, torment, and hurt you are feeling, you suck it up and keep smiling for the world. You're not going to let anyone see you down and out. The last thing anyone wants to feel like is a failure, especially in a relationship. Girl, stop it. Let that stuff go. Don't worry about what others think of you, because everyone has an opinion, and what they think of you has nothing to do with you. And stop trying to please folks. Please yourself first.

What Rachel and so many other women don't know is that you are not failures because a relationship did not work. The relationship did not work simply because it didn't work. That's all that happened. Making sense of why it ended is not going to help you in the healing process, because you will find every excuse in the book of why it's your fault. Then, when you get tired of beating up on yourself, you will begin to beat up on the man. And girl, haven't we all beaten up on the many men in our lives at one time or another?

Once your anger is redirected towards the man, you will call up all your girlfriends, rounding up the troops to have a man-bashing party. You will talk about all his negative traits and the wrongs he did during the relationship. You will enumerate all his faults and shortcomings. Things you clearly saw in the beginning of the relationship, but chose to ignore.

Here is something that is vital to move on with your life and start the healing process—forgive yourself. *Let it go.* It was a lesson learned. This man was not the one for you. But until you forgive yourself, you will not be open to receive the blessing of a new man in your life.

Just imagine being out on a date, and all you talk about is what "Michael," "Eric," "John," or "Kyle" did to you. These men messed over you. They lied, cheated, and got away with it for a while, until you caught them. But by the time you discovered their infidelity and trifling ways, they were already romantically linked to other women. Being the better person that you are, you just burned up their clothes, destroyed their property, called them every name but a child of God, and told their mommas what they did to you. (Sort of like the moment in the movie *Waiting To Exhale*, when Angela Bassett's character discovers her husband is leaving her. She piles all his clothes into his Mercedes-Benz, pours gasoline on it, and sets it ablaze. It was a fierce scene, for the movies, but not one to re-create in real life).

When women are emotionally hurt by a man, some refuse to let the relationship end, because they do not want to let go of the pain he has caused. They want him to feel what they are feeling. Instead of forgiving herself, or him, a woman will do anything to get a reaction from their ex.

Some of you are so compelled, you want to cause physical harm and attack him or even the other woman he is involved with. I've seen it happen, too. Women jump on the other woman. Fighting like some young middle-school girls. Just plain ole' silliness. One, you are too old for that. Two, *you are too old for that*. And three, *you are still too damned old for that*! I will take away all your Diva points!

Besides, when you decide to act out in an unwomanly manner, that sort of behavior can lead to arrest and public humiliation. Which could lead to losing a job, money, or having to spend some time in jail. Really, is it worth it? Is *he* worth it?

Don't let temporary insanity happen to you.

You are a lady. A woman. A Diva. And as your Gay Best Friend, I will not allow you to indulge in such immature impulses. Besides, you will mess up a good manicure and weave. Learn to forgive and move on.

I know ending a relationship is emotionally draining. And it is important for you to take the time to experience and feel the hurt and pain. But don't let an entire month or year go by still mulling over the relationship.

Right now I want you to close your eyes and relax. Acknowledge you are hurting. I want you to feel what that hurt is doing to you, physically, emotionally and mentally. Breathe in and breathe out. Don't think about that man. I know he popped up in your head. Stop it!

Now, close your eyes again and relax. Take deep breaths in. Slowly count to three and then exhale. Do it once more. Actually, do it a few more times.

Now, don't you feel better? I know I do.

Don't allow yourself to live in the pain and hurt. Do other positive things to move on. Read the Bible or other books that lift your Spirit. Listen to inspirational music, or find some events to get involved with that inspire you. Dress up, go out, party, and have fun. Don't sit around moping trying to figure out what he's doing and with whom. It is imperative to nurture your own Spirit and allow yourself time to heal.

Most ladies will ignore the inner voice and Spirit and rush into another relationship to get over the man who did them wrong. They never allow themselves the opportunity to heal. All of the pain, hurt, and bitterness are carried into the new relationship.

In the beginning of a new relationship, you will do everything possible to not compare your new man to your previous boyfriend. However, the real person, the real you, will eventually show up. Yes, Girl, everything you are trying to hide will be revealed, including the hurt and the pain. And as your Gay Best Friend, I am here to tell you it is not cute, appealing, or enticing. You cannot do anything about it, however, because your Spirit needs to purge, and if you are not conscious of your own spiritual development, you will find yourself complaining, crying at odd times, and slowly pushing the new man out of your life. A perpetual cycle you'll never get out of.

Take, for example, Grammy Award-winning songstress and the Queen of Hip-Hop Soul, Mary J. Blige.

For years, Mary has lived her life in the public eye. We've seen her go through drug and alcohol abuse. We've been with her through her tumultuous relationships, be they physical or emotional. We watched from the sidelines as she experienced heartache and let it all out through her music. Many of you even sat in dark rooms of your homes with whole bottles of wine, singing your hearts out with Mary J. Blige. I know I did, especially with her album *My Life*. My cocktail glass was on a constant flow of vodka with that album. I swear, Mary was singing the tunes of my very own life. We were all right there in the moment with her. Mary understood our pain.

Mary poured her heart and soul onto those tracks, letting all of us know how she felt about the men in her life—the men who mistreated, abused, and used her.

Mary was open about the pain she was experiencing. The pain from her childhood of not having a father in the home, witnessing the domestic abuse heaped on her mother by boyfriends. These childhood experiences led Mary to become destructive and chaotic in her own life. Drugs and alcohol became her coping mechanisms. Suicidal tendencies loomed at her doorstep. Her life was spiraling out of control.

Many of you have probably had similar problems. You came from a single-parent home, or your parents fought nonstop. You vowed you would never let that happen to you. Then you met the first man who turned your life upside down and broke your heart. It has been one man after another ever since. No matter how hard you've tried, you end up in disastrous and dysfunctional relationships, one after another. Each man uses and takes from you, leaving you depleted and empty. You're tired of being tired. No more Ms. Nice Woman.

So, you decide you're going to behave just like the men, and treat them just like they have treated you. Or you decide to become celibate and not have sex until you meet the right man. If a man doesn't treat you like the queen you feel you are, then you put up a wall and prevent him from getting close to you emotionally or physically. This is the end of you being a doormat for men. No justice, no piece—he will have no piece of you in any way, shape, or form.

This leads to the second step of forgiveness, which is to forgive the man or men you feel did you wrong. That's correct. You need to forgive him (or them).

Girl, I know it's going to be hard, but please hear me out on this one. Forgive him because he only did what he knew how to do. He only did what you allowed him to do. That man was operating from his own background of dysfunction—and two dysfunctional people in a relationship is an unhealthy mix. Besides, his exposure to you was probably too much for him. Or maybe it was not enough. He probably couldn't handle a strong and independent woman. You've got your own things—money, car, house, clothes, and jewelry. What could he possibly bring to the table? Maybe he wasn't ready to be treated like a child again. Your smothering and motherly characteristics might have pushed him away.

Whatever the case may have been, forgive him. He was placed in your life to teach you a lesson. Be grateful and forgive him.

Trust me when I tell you this. If you don't forgive him, you will carry this man's energy into every relationship you have.

*Forgive us of our trespasses as we forgive those who trespass against us* (Matthew 6:12).

Mary J. Blige matured and grew spiritually. She speaks openly and candidly about the power of forgiveness. Instead of being bitter and angry, she learned to forgive all the men in her life who had treated her wrong. She also took responsibility for the part she played. She stopped being the victim and became the *victor*. She reclaimed her Spirit and her life. Mary took control and opened herself for Spirit to guide her. She listened and is now in a loving and happy relationship with a man who nurtures and supports her.

Yes, this too can be you. You can be happy. You can be in a loving relationship. You can have the man for you.

So stop being unwilling to forgive. Sure, it *does* hurt when a relationship is over. It is painful to endure a heartbreak after a man you hoped you would be with forever suddenly ends it. We *all* want the long-lasting love. We all want to be desired and needed by someone. However, to get love, you must forgive all your past hurts and let him go.

We question Spirit sometimes, because we meet someone and they do something to us we don't understand. They come into our lives and disrupt our journey. They make us laugh when we want to cry. They make us feel when we want to shut down. They make us do things we normally wouldn't do, and we get caught up in them and their lives. We live and breathe for them. Yet they take, and take, and take. They are only doing what they know how to do—and that may be their purpose.

Let it go. Let him go. Girl, just let go!

I was in Washington, DC for a workshop when I came across a very beautiful woman, "Katherine." I could tell she didn't *think* she was beautiful by the way she held her head down. Her long luxurious hair was tied up in a ponytail. Her body was hidden in frumpy baggy jeans and an oversized sweater. (I tell you, these women really wear me out with their fashions. It hurts my gayness to see women looking shabby and blasé.)

Katherine waited patiently as I shook hands and spoke with the line of women ahead of her. When it was finally her turn, I motioned for her to come over. She seemed apprehensive, but I flashed my smile at her and she blushed.

Katherine asked if we could speak somewhere privately. She didn't want a lot of people around when she told me her story.

"I really feel like I don't know what to do," she said to me. "I'm tired of being mistreated and used. I want to take back my life."

We found a corner in the large room and sat down. I looked into Katherine's large brown eyes. She looked as if her life had been a series of ups and downs. "I don't know where to begin," she said looking down and wringing her hands.

"Well, why don't you start at the beginning," I said.

She began to tell me the story about "Jason," a man who had done her terribly wrong. She went on to tell me about how he mistreated her. They had been in a relationship for three years and she had hoped to marry this man. They were living together in her apartment.

"We have our share of problems, but we always work through them," she said looking at me for confirmation that everyone did have problems in their relationships. I said nothing.

"My mother told me that men are going to be men," Katherine continued. "She always told me, you've got to let some things slide and learn to pick your battles." Katherine confessed she chose *not* to battle. "I saw my mother marry and divorce three different men. I don't want that to be my life. I don't want to end up like my mother. I just want to be with one man, and only one man."

Tears formed in the corners of her dark brown eyes. I reached over and touched her shoulder. "It's okay," I said.

I wanted to hear the full story before I laid down the law and whipped out my glass full of Big Stick (I am not saying anything, but a Big Stick goes a long way).

"I know sometimes you have to stand by your man despite how hard the times get," Katherine lifted her head and stared into my eyes. "I don't want to come across as the angry or jilted girlfriend, so I never berate or argue with Jason. I've seen too many women lose their men because they have that *I-don't-need-a-man syndrome*."

I gave her a simple look and stopped myself from rolling my eyes. Was she really serious? But then again, I knew she was.

I know lots of women who have the *I-don't-need-a-man syndrome*. It's so sad. They degrade, beat up, and talk about men like dogs, yet they are always complaining they can't find a man. They can't find a man to be good to them, love them, hold them, and be a man for them. (Well, sweetie, if you let go of the bitterness then maybe, just maybe, you can meet a man who will be good to you.)

Katherine then told me she never thought of herself as pretty enough. "I am always comparing myself to other women. It's the way I look, my body, clothes, and hair. Sometimes I just don't want to look at myself."

Now, Katherine wasn't unattractive, and she didn't appear to be an overweight woman. I couldn't really tell because of those hideous clothes she was hiding under. (Instead of sitting there talking, we should have been out shopping and discussing all of this over fashion. Imagine it, talking about men and shopping at all your favorite stores. There is absolutely nothing better than going through racks and racks of clothes, and shoes. Don't you just love it? But I had to refocus and get Bloomingdale's, Barneys, and Saks out of my mind. I had to *focus.*)

So, when the thought of Jason possibly cheating entered Katherine's mind, she dismissed it. "He always compliments other women on television and in the magazines. I know I can't compete with those women. They are beautiful and have gorgeous bodies."

"Well, you know what, Katherine, you can't compete with those women. They are beautiful and have gorgeous bodies," I said. She jerked her head back and raised her brows.

"First and foremost, the women in the magazines are airbrushed," I said. "Their pictures are retouched to make them look abnormally beautiful. And the women on television have their imperfections covered up as well. They know how to stand to hide certain body parts that are unflattering. They know what their best angles are to disguise the blemishes on their faces and other imperfections. They have stylists and makeup artists working on them to make them look camera-ready. Unfortunately, you don't have a glam squad, so girl, stop comparing yourself." Katherine chuckled. I then reached for her hair and untied her ponytail. Her black hair fell on her shoulders and down her back.

"Damn, girl! You got some hair on you. Why are you hiding it on that pretty little head of yours?" Katherine blushed.

I could tell she started to feel better about herself. She teased her hair and a smile swept across her face.

She continued her story, revealing how she had developed part of her low self-esteem by not being "enough" in previous relationships with men who cheated on her. Katherine carried this baggage from one relationship right into another, even now with Jason. "I became very mistrustful of the men who cheated on me, but I remained in the relationships as long as they promised to not let it happen again. I felt like I was being supportive and understanding."

I restrained my tongue from giving her lashing. I prayed I wouldn't let my slip of the tongue say something that would damage her already bruised self-esteem.

Her previous boyfriends had told her she was not generally the type of girl they dated. "They said I was nice-looking, but I wasn't a knockout. That was a blow to me. I hated hearing those words. It made me feel unworthy, and as if they'd settled for me. I know I deserve better. I deserve goodness, but I just don't know how to get it."

I knelt before her and took her hands in mine. It was now time for me to be her Gay Best Friend.

"You *do* deserve goodness. You *do* deserve better, but girl, *you've* got to love you first. If *you* don't love you, then it is impossible to have someone else love you."

Katherine had stayed in those relationships because she wanted to make them work. She thought her boyfriends would eventually see how committed and dedicated she was to them, and somehow, or some way, they would change their minds about her.

It didn't work.

Now Katherine was in her current relationship with Jason, trying to make it work. Again.

Katherine let out a huge sigh. "I let him move in because he was between jobs. He doesn't have a car, so I let him use mine while I am at work. He isn't a bad boyfriend; he just can't seem to make things work for himself."

"Well, one day I left work early because I wasn't feeling well. Jason didn't answer his cell phone, the one I bought for him," Katherine jabbed her finger into her chest. Her voice was escalating. (Yeah, she was going there. She was getting loud and the pain was pushing through her vocals. She was finding her inner Diva voice. Her inner gay.)

"I was calling him to let him know to come pick me up. After four attempts, I just took the bus home. And do you know what happened when I walked through the door?" She asked with her eyes wide and her hands on her hips. I shook my head. "There he was. That good-for-nothing son of a bitch was in my apartment, in my bed with another woman. I lost it. I simply lost it and went ballistic. I threw both of them out." Her breathing was rapid. Her chest was heaving up and down.

"Well, good for you!" I exclaimed.

"But how did I allow myself to get into this situation again? How could this happen to me?" She dropped her head. I lifted her chin with my hand.

"We don't mope over men," I said.

I know many of you are asking the same questions as Katherine. What happened? How did you end up in this situation again?

Well, in Katherine's case, it happened because she refused to forgive herself from the past relationships when she allowed men to abuse her. She didn't learn the lesson. Just like many of you.

Katherine never forgave herself or the men she let use and mistreat her. She never forgave herself because she felt she deserved the treatment. Katherine didn't place any value on her self-worth. She didn't want to be seen as the bad girlfriend who didn't trust her man, so she went along just to get along.

If she had been stronger, mentally and emotionally, then she wouldn't have allowed herself to be mistreated by her previous boyfriends. Katherine was just happy to have a man. Especially because all her friends were single and looked at her relationships as some sign of hope for themselves.

Katherine had to learn to forgive herself for allowing herself to feel like a victim. She had to learn to love herself enough to know she was worthy. Unfortunately, no one ever told her of that.

It was my duty as her Gay Best Friend to remind her she was worthy. She was enough. She was Miss It!

I also had to teach her to forgive the men who had mistreated and abused her. They only did what she allowed them to do. She let them get away with mistreating her without any repercussions. She had no boundaries in what she allowed her previous boyfriends to do to her. She certainly didn't think she was deserving of love or of someone being good to her.

If you think you are trash, then you will *get* trash. If you think you are nothing, then you will meet people who will bring nothing to the table. Whatever you think about yourself is exactly what you will experience.

*As a man thinketh in his heart, so is he* (Proverbs 23:7).

You see, Katherine didn't like herself much, and the first man who came along and showed her any type of affection, it felt good to her. She liked it and refused to recognize the many signs blaring and blinking in red neon lights right in front of her. And many others are guilty of the same thing. You romanticize relationships into something they aren't. Thinking the ill-behavior is cute.

Darling, it isn't cute. It's time to look at things the way they are, and not the way you hope they will be.

Also, despite Katherine being a size ten, almost every other month she was on a different diet—Atkins, South Beach, Master Cleanse, the no-carbs diet.

And don't sit there reading this with a disgusted look on your face when you know damn well you've tried the same diets, or at least thought about it. (Hell, I've done *all* of them. Had some wonderful successes, but I'll be damned if I didn't gain the weight back, plus some. Yes, ladies, we have a lot more in common than you think—men, weight, love, and clothes.)

Anyway, Katherine hated her body, and she was glad she could hide in her nurse's uniform. Friends complimented her on her figure, but her boyfriends nitpicked at her.

The men would ask, "Why don't you ever dress sexy? You should do something with yourself."

Katherine just kept herself busy with her career. It was her salvation, her escape. At work, no one cared what she looked like. She was in a hospital, working with the sick, and they surely didn't care about her physical appearance, just as long as she took care of them and helped them recover from whatever was ailing them.

Listen, ladies, I don't care what type of job you have, you'd better walk up in the place looking *fierce,* with all eyes on you. Don't let clothes drown you out by hiding your thighs, ass, hips, and breasts. If you got it, flaunt it. Work what you've got!

There are many Katherines out there, and many of you can relate to her story. You may be in a relationship like Katherine's.

What are you going to do about it?

Sometimes Spirit will send someone to you to see if you are ready for the greatness Spirit has in store for you. Sometimes Spirit is checking to see if you can recognize someone you said you would not be with. You know exactly what I'm talking about. The man who smoked or drank, whom you said you would not date. The man who didn't want to have children, whom you said you would not date.

Take a moment to remember what you have promised to yourself. Do you remember your criteria for the man you said you wanted to be with? You probably have not thought about it, because when the first man came along, you said to yourself that you could compromise. It was something you could deal with. You told yourself that over time, he could change.

It didn't happen, did it? Now, forgive yourself.

Here is something simple you can do for yourself to forgive. Ask yourself if the stress of holding on to an unhealthy relationship is worth it. Ask yourself if holding on to the pain is worth it.

Now, ask yourself if happiness, joy, and love are worth it.

Then ask yourself for the lesson and what you have learned.

Here's another exercise you can do. Each morning, afternoon, or evening go to the mirror and affirm yourself. Forgive yourself. Tell yourself how much you love you. Forgive the man who hurt you. Forgive him and let him go. Smile at yourself and always remember—you are loved, loving, and lovable simply because I, your Gay Best Friend, says so. And so does God.

Now. Let's raise our glasses and have a toast! Here's to the new you. The Diva you are. And to all the fabulousness you are destined to be. CHEERS!

# Chapter 11

# Be Still and Wait: Patience Is a Virtue

Anything worth having is worth waiting for. When you are looking for something for your home or your yard or your wardrobe, you take your time and shop around. You don't jump on the first thing you see. You browse, look, and then go home and think it over. The same rule applies when you are looking to date. You have to be still and wait.

If you have doubts or concerns about a particular man, just be still and wait. He will reveal his true colors in time.

Pull up a chair beside me, Diva-cakes. Let me pour you a drink. How about a Strawberry Storm? It's better than a Blue Monday.

Now, I have the belief that if you listen carefully to someone when you meet him, he will tell you all you will ever need to know about him in fifteen minutes. It doesn't take three, six, or twelve months to discover something about someone that he made perfectly clear when you first met him.

It pains me when I hear some women say after things go wrong, "I didn't know he could be like that." Or "I thought he was different." Girl, most likely he told you who he was when you first met him. If you had been paying attention, you would have heard and seen all the signs.

Let me say it again. Ladies, when people tell you who they are, *believe them.*

If they tell you they are crazy, then, guess what? They are crazy.

If they tell you they are obnoxious, then, guess what? They are obnoxious.

It's like your mother always told you: *If it quacks like a duck, walks like a duck, and talks like a duck, then, guess what? It's a duck.*

I remember when I was at a house party some years back. I met this guy, and he and I flirted heavily with one another. It was playful and fun. I introduced myself and told him my name. I then asked him for his. He replied saying, "Drama." Seriously, I am not lying. That is how he introduced himself.

I politely shook his hand and said, "Thanks, but no thanks. I am not looking for any."

He stood there with a look of shock on his face as I turned and walked away. I guess he assumed I was joking, but I was not. I was serious. Within those few minutes he told me who he was. I believed him and went on my merry way.

But I know that some ladies (and men) in the same situation would have laughed, flirted, and continued talking up a storm. They would have ignored everything he said and thrown caution to the wind. Why not, when he is fine and he is flirting with you?

Girl, please.

It's inevitable for us as humans to pay attention to those things that our Spirit would pick up on quickly. However, if you are not paying attention, and you're thinking with your body because it's calling for some attention, you will get a man that you did not bargain for.

To avoid all the drama, pain, and aggravation (and I know it's difficult, especially when you think you will not meet the man for you), just be still and wait. He will show up at the right time.

In my book *Reclaim Your Power!* I talk about how, in order to listen and hear Spirit speaking, you have to be still. We are so caught up in our busy lives and schedules that we do not make the time to be still long enough to even hear ourselves think.

When you are anxious to be in a relationship with a man, you avoid listening to yourself and Spirit. A man can show up and seem to be the one for you, but until you are still and take the time to get to know him, you will not find out everything you need to know.

Rushing into a relationship with any man is not good for your life or health. It can cause you pain, hurt, and bitterness, and you could have avoided it all if you had just *been still* and waited.

My good friend, Kevin E. Taylor, who is a pastor, and I were talking about relationships and how impatient we as humans are. "We are so desperate to be with someone, we take the first thing coming and try to make it work," Rev. Kevin said. "We spend a lot of time trying to fix and shape them into the person we want them to be. Or we compromise our morals and beliefs just to say that we have somebody."

That sounds ludicrous doesn't it? I said the same thing.

Rev. Kevin then told me this great analogy. "As we grow in our spiritual walk, we climb higher on the mountain of grace," he said. "Each stop on the mountain is a temporary place, because we are to keep growing and keep climbing to our greatest potential. As you are climbing the mountain of grace you encounter other folks along the way. Some have stopped climbing because they just can't seem to go any further. There are those who are resting and need a boost, so you provide them with some spiritual food and they continue on. Then there are those who are super-climbers. They are always looking to get to the next place because they are excited about the journey and they love the discovery of new things on the mountain.

"When you are at your rest stop on the mountain, you begin to take inventory of what's there with you. You notice that there may not be any other people on the same journey or place you are. When you don't see anyone, you begin to feel out of place and alone. You begin to doubt the journey and think the rest of the climb will be just the same.

"When it doesn't seem as if anyone will join you, you climb back down the mountain and go back to the valley you left to find someone. You go back to a place you left where you know there is no growth. You are back in the valley looking for your man. While you are there, you resort to some of your old habits and behaviors.

Before you know it, you have been back in the valley for three to six months.

"While you were down in the valley, guess what? The man for you *did* show up at the place you left, higher up on the mountain. But because you could not be still and wait, you missed him. You missed the man who was growing and climbing the mountain of grace. The man you have been searching and asking for came for you, and now you have missed him. You don't know it because you are trapped back down in the valley.

"After your time in the valley, you decide to get back on the journey to the mountaintop and you attempt to bring the man you found in the valley with you. When you bring the man you met from the valley on the journey to the mountaintop, he's not equipped to handle the pressure and climb, nor is he ready to be out of the valley. So now you are back to where you started asking the same question: 'Why can't I seem to find a man for me?'"

That's powerful, isn't it?

It's an old habit and pattern. We all do it. We think that we won't find anyone on our journey as we continue to grow spiritually. Self-doubt leaves us fearful and without hope. This will keep us repeating and doing things we swore we'd never do again.

Believe me, Ms. Honey, it is lonely on this walk sometimes, but whatever God has in store for you, no man can prevent it from happening.

Learn to stop getting in your own way and preventing your blessings from happening. I know you get tired of doing things alone, but you have to know this is all preparation. If you can enjoy your own company, then the man for you will enjoy being in your presence. He will see that you are having a good time and will thoroughly like sharing his time and energy with you.

I hope after reading this next story you will see the benefits of being still and waiting.

I remember a woman I met at a workshop in Kentucky. "Sandra" was in a huge mess. It was a big bind.

Sandra was a very spiritual Christian woman. Her presence glowed with it, but her heart and mind were heavy. She waited nearly an hour just to talk to me.

"Terrance, I need your advice," Sandra said. "I've prayed and asked God, but I want to talk it out with you. I feel as if my life is spinning out of control."

"Of course," I said. I saw the pain in her eyes. I grabbed her by the hand and we went outside to a nearby park where we sat on a bench. "Tell me what's going on," I said.

"Well, a while back, my teenage daughter and I had just moved into a nice newly developed suburban community. I had just purchased my first home and I was so excited. The Lord was truly working in my life.

"I started seeing a man who was also a Christian, but he had a very dark past. He is a former drug dealer, hustler, and user who had been to prison, but he had turned his life over to God and was in ministerial school studying to become a minister."

I nodded my head, because that sounded wonderful.

"We had dated years back and broken up. But he resurfaced and we decided to give it a go again," Sandra said. "I know everything about his past. The women, children, child-support payments, prison stints, him being on parole, and him going through a divorce with his second wife. But he was a renewed man. I was happy to be a part of his life. I was happy that he was doing something with his life and working on letting go of bad habits. He had a stable job making good money and he had just recently purchased his own beautiful home in a neighboring nice suburban area. He was doing really well for himself.

"We had only been back together for three months when he told me that God had spoken to him and said that I am supposed to be his wife. Terrance, I was so excited. I had been praying and waiting on a man. It had been a year since I had been praying faithfully and asking God to send me a man. But for some odd reason God had not spoken to me."

This is where I sat up and gave her a look like she was crazy.

I was thinking, *He told you that God spoke to him and said you are supposed to be his wife? Girl, you fell for that?*

Don't get me wrong. I do believe God speaks to people. Every day. But her story sounded really fishy. Still, I held my tongue and continued listening.

"He proposed marriage and I accepted," Sandra said. "I then switched churches and joined my fiancé's church, where he was seeking to become a deacon. We went to the pastor of his church and the pastor told us that he would not officiate our wedding. He felt it was too soon. The pastor also did not put my fiancé on his staff. He wanted to wait and see my fiancé's spiritual walk become much stronger."

Now, girl, if that isn't a clue I don't know what is.

But I refrained from speaking because Sandra wasn't done.

"My fiancé said my daughter and I had to move into his house with him and we would still get married. He said moving into his house would help cut down on the costs of two mortgages, especially his since he was working and going to school.

"I was skeptical because I had just bought my home. I would have to find someone to rent out my home. I knew the process would be long and tedious, yet I still was not sure if that was the right thing to do. Something in my gut didn't feel right, but I didn't want to argue with my fiancé because he said God had spoken to him.

"Well, out of the blue, and a month later, my Realtor found someone to rent the home. I thought maybe it was a sign from God. Maybe it was meant to be. However, my daughter was upset. She didn't want to move. In fact, she wanted to move with her father rather than move in with my fiancé.

"My daughter and I fought over it, but she ultimately moved in with me and my fiancé. Everything was wonderful for the first two months. He eventually got a divorce from his second wife. We got married at my old church, since his pastor would not marry us, and I took his last name. Things were perfect for a few months.

"Well, one day I discovered my husband was still going to see his ex-wife and other ex-girlfriends. I found out he was selling drugs and hustling again. I also found a box of letters and pictures of all the women he had been with in his past."

I needed a drink. At that moment, a Jamaican Me Crazy sounded just about perfect.

I truly couldn't believe the story, let alone that Sandra was really that caught up in a man. Desperation is a distinct perfume and a man who's seeking a woman will smell it from ten miles away. Sandra was *doused* in it.

I was itching to release a fierce tongue-lashing, but Sandra had more.

Yes, she had more to tell.

And it gets more interesting.

"I was pissed," Sandra continued. "I couldn't believe all this was going on and I didn't see it. I couldn't understand what was happening and why it was happening to me. So I confronted him, in public, at the barbershop, in front of all his friends. He tried to deny it, but I had the pictures in my hand. I threw them at him, spat in his face, and left him standing there. I then went back to the house and waited on him. I was going to give him some more of my mind.

"Well, he walked in and everything hit the fan. We argued and yelled. He finally confessed to everything. He then told me that I was his wife and I was not to disrespect him and that I had to follow his rules. He quoted scriptures from the Bible where it stated a woman should be submissive to a man. He told me I had been out in the world too long and that I wasn't used to a man telling me what to do. We argued for a few hours, and then we had sex."

I know you are shaking your head as you read this story.

I was convulsing.

Yet there is still more.

"My husband told me he was going to see his exes because he wanted to get advice on what to do in his marriage. He was struggling and he said they provided support for him. He also admitted to going back to selling drugs and hustling, and he said, *'God knows my heart.'*

"I consulted the church and my friends about what to do. I prayed and asked God what to do. I needed some answers. I needed help.

"Things proceeded to get even worse. My husband stayed out late and sometimes didn't come home at all. I started worrying and began to lose sleep, weight, and almost my job. Everything finally came to a head. After five months of marriage, I decided to get a divorce. I couldn't take it any longer. And you know what? He didn't care. He was not bothered.

"The divorce was messy. Our business was out in the streets. My husband went back to his ex-wife and started sleeping with her. He asked me and my daughter to move out so his ex-wife could move in.

"I have recently met another man. He is so supportive and nurturing. He wants to move me and my daughter with him into his home."

Ladies, ooh, I can see your faces and hear you now.

What is *wrong* with this woman? Is she *serious*? Let me get to her and I'll tell her a few things.

You have to know when to have tough love with some people, and others you have to empathize and be patient with them. As a Gay Best Friend, I knew how to gauge this situation and I decided to proceed with caution, because Sandra was blind and oblivious to the truth of her situation.

I stood up and walked over to a tree where I steadied myself. I said a silent prayer. *Lord, give me the strength and words to be kind and loving with Sandra, because if I let loose my tongue I am going to hurt her feelings.*

I then went back to the bench where Sandra was sitting staring at me confused. "What's wrong?" She asked.

"Sandra, I am in shock right now. Your story has really taken the cake. I've heard some stories, and believe me they have been some traumatic experiences, but, girl, you win." I sat down and looked Sandra in the eyes.

"I am going to be very loving and very serious with you. I need for you to really look at your situation and determine if you are really ready to move on in a new relationship with another man so soon. You have to think how this is not only affecting you, but your daughter as well. I am sure she is traumatized from your recent relationship. She is being thrust in these situations because you are looking for love in all the wrong places.

"I understand your situation and why you felt compelled to marry your current ex-husband. You knew him. The two of you had history together. When he came back in your life you felt comfortable. That's what old blankets, shoes, and clothes do to you. They form to you and fit like a glove. They are familiar and you like things that are familiar."

(And ladies, don't act like you haven't had a man you'd dated return to your life, and you tried it again and it didn't work again.)

Anyway, I continued with Sandra.

I asked her, "Why didn't you trust yourself when you had heard in your own heart that he was not the man for you to marry? Ms. Honey, *think* about why his pastor refused to marry you. Why do you think his own pastor, of his own church, did not invite your ex-husband to join his staff, and he questioned his spiritual walk?"

She couldn't answer me. I could tell she was still caught up in why her ex-husband did her so wrong.

"Terrance, I hear you but, why did he have me and my daughter move out of my house that I just bought, and move into his?" She started fuming and seething. Her eyes grew tight, as well as her lips. "He didn't have to do this to us. Why play games like that? And now he is going back to his ex-wife, and he asked her to move in. I hate him!"

I shook my head. No matter what I was about to say, Sandra wouldn't hear me. She was caught up in her anger. And you know what they say about an angry woman: *Hell has no fury like a woman scorned.*

Sandra was angry, hurt, and in a fragile state of mind. No one could get through to Sandra to help her to see *what* had happened to her and *why* it had happened to her. She was going to have to pray to God for answers, seek guidance from her pastor, and hopefully discover the pattern she was in and creating.

I told Sandra that she should take some time to be alone.

She hated that answer. She had been alone for a year. Sandra wanted to be in a relationship. She asked for my number so she could reach out to me if she had any further questions.

It only took me a quick second to think about it before I told her I could give her my e-mail address. "That would be the best way to correspond with me," I said to Sandra.

(I seriously hope y'all didn't think I would give her my number. I refuse to be a part of people's pity parties, "He did me wrong. What should I do? Why can't I meet a man?" No ma'am. Not The Kid. I am not going to be on the phone with you for hours listening to that mess. Girl, I may be your Gay Best Friend, but I am not your therapist, counselor, or pastor. I will only give you one good cry-over-the-phone-moping session, after that, I am going to lay into you and give it to you straight. It's my job.)

I heard from Sandra a few months later by e-mail. She wrote that she had not moved in with the new man who was pursuing her, but they were still dating. She went back to her church home and had started therapy with a psychologist. Her daughter was happy, and Sandra said she was starting to feel good about herself.

She did also say that her ex-husband had been reaching out to her to reconcile, but she didn't think it was a good idea. Well, her actual words were, "It will be a cold day in hell before I get back with that bum."

I was happy she was in therapy, but from the tone of her e-mail I knew she had a ways to go on her journey. I was proud she recognized she needed professional help, and I responded to Sandra that she could e-mail me any time.

Divas, I want you to know patience is a virtue when you are looking to seriously date a man. It would do many of you good to practice it. Rushing into any situation is not wise or healthy. God is always patiently working, molding, and shaping you into your greatness. Even when you stray off the path and do what you want to do, God's spirit is always waiting patiently for you to come back home. There are no questions.

Before you leap into any ol' relationship with any ol' man, take time to be with yourself and to develop your Spirit, mind, and body. Remember that the race is not given to the swiftest, but to those who can endure the journey.

# Chapter 12

# Be Open to Love When It Shows Up:
# A Closed Heart Doesn't Receive Joy

Some women want a Prince Charming or a knight in shining armor to come and save the day. Some just want a simple man. A man who works, takes care of the home, loves his children, and is spiritually grounded.

Whatever you need from a man, when you ask Spirit for him, you have to be open to receiving love when it shows up. When you ask God for your man, you have to be prepared. There's no use asking for him if you're not ready when he comes. You can't start running around trying to fix your hair, dress, makeup, and attitude *after* he arrives. Be prepared for your man, especially with an open heart and willingness to accept him.

I'm telling you, I've heard *lots* of women complain about the good guy. You know the one. The man who is extremely nice, a gentleman, loves children, practices chivalry, and is spiritually grounded. He has a good head on his shoulders and will love you like no other. However, there's always a catch. He is not tall enough, or dark enough. He may be a blue-collar worker. He may be younger than you, maybe even older.

I swear, Diva, sometimes I think most women only want the thug, or wannabe thug brother who has a criminal record, bad credit, emotional issues, and can't maintain a job. Something about fixing a brother up seems to intrigue these women. They want to feel like they are the ones responsible for helping him see the light, get back on his feet, and turn his life around. Despite the fact that he got them into debt, ruined their credit, and caused them several nervous breakdowns.

Girl, bye!

I hear women say all the time, "There's just something about a bad boy. The swagger in his step. The chip on his shoulder and his arrogance. He's confident and bold. He won't just make love to me. He'll also fulfill my sexual fantasies and desires."

I mean, really.

Do these women really think it's going to be lilies in the field, days at the park, and chilling at the beachfront all the time? Men like that only exists in movies. Filmmakers and screenwriters create these characters as fantasy. But these women—otherwise sane, with-it, together women—think these characters are *real*. They daydream about Morris Chestnut, Boris Kodjoe, and Idris Elba sweeping them off their feet.

Wake up, my little mutton chop, and come back to Earth.

If you keep looking for Mr. Do-Me-Bad-Boy, then you will miss out on a plethora of eligible men. Mr. Right will show up right in front of your eyes, but your blinders will prevent you from seeing what's directly in front of you.

Some women ask for love but are not willing to accept it when it shows up. That's telling Spirit, "Thanks, but no thanks. I do deserve love, but I want it *my way*."

Love may be knocking at your door, but you can't hear it with closed ears and a closed heart.

When you are not used to love from a man who is able to express himself, or a man who rubs your back and feet when you get home, or a man who cooks and cleans for you, you start saying, "This is too good to be true" when he comes into your life. Even though you have asked for him, you can't believe he is actually there.

It reminds me of Lauryn Hill's album *The Miseducation of Lauryn Hill*. During the interlude, a few adults are asking the young students in the classroom about love. One of the students, a young woman, says, "If you've never been in love before, then you don't know what it's like to be loved."

---

That was so powerful coming from a young woman.

She apparently already knows, at an early age, that if you've never experienced love, then you wouldn't know the feeling of being in love.

If you close yourself off from the feeling of being in love, then you are missing out on one of God's greatest gifts.

Look at the R&B singer, Beyoncé, and the rap artist, Jay-Z. Beyoncé is one the most beautiful and admired women in the world—talented, smart, and could probably have any man she wants. Yet, she found love and happiness with someone whom many may feel is beneath her.

I am not one to judge anyone, nor tell anyone whom they should love. People fall in love all the time with folks who many would never imagine they would. And I have had my share of men who were less than desirable. After a few drinks (okay, a bottle of liquor) they are very attractive. When you come to your less-than-inebriated senses, however, you can't believe you are sleeping with him.

Don't sit there like you don't know the man I am talking about.

You will creep over to his house in the middle of the night. *Real* late at night. I mean *really, really* late at night. You don't tell any of your friends about him, because you are too embarrassed of what they may say.

But that man loves everything about you.

Maybe you are *not* ashamed of your new man. However, I am certain that at some point or time in your life, people questioned your judgment about your boyfriend. And you probably stood by his side and defended him.

But many women are shallow. They would let their friends talk them out of dating someone who could be their future husband or life partner. (Don't act like your friends have not influenced your decisions on your man at some point.)

Think about the not-so-good-looking-man who loves your dirty drawers. He is a perfect gentleman and can put it *down* in the bedroom. You only see him at night. You go to his house because you don't want anyone to see him entering your home. He asks you out on dates and you come up with every excuse in the book why you are not available.

You would not be caught dead in public with him.

Yet this man loves the ground you walk on. He worships you and will do anything for you. But because you think your friends and family members will laugh you under a rock for being with someone they might not find acceptable on the surface, you tuck him away in a dark closet like an old piece of clothing.

Shame, shame, *shame.*

I remember this R&B song that recording artists Babyface and Pebbles recorded together in 1990—"Love Makes Things Happen." This sing epitomizes the idea that you never know who you will fall in love with.

You have no control over love.

Let me tell you about this woman, "June," who is in her late thirties, whom I know in New York City.

June is a fabulous stylist for the stars, and she was one of my newest hanging buddies. I met her while I was dating a former stylist for one of hip-hop's biggest moguls and artists. June and I hit it off. She has a bubbly personality, and her outward appearance was flawless.

We were hanging out at a dinner party and chatting over a delicious serving of rice and peas and oxtails. June loves to eat and has no qualms letting that fact be known. (That's the type of woman I love being with. Let's eat some wonderful food along with our Conjure Cognac!)

While we were stuffing our faces, June and I became engrossed in a deep conversation. She revealed to me that she was sorry for dumping a man who had once loved her. When she was in her twenties, June had met this amazing man. And according to her, "It was magical. This man was everything a woman could ask for."

June stopped eating. I noticed sadness in her eyes. I listened intently, assessing her mood. I heard a little resentment, but before I made a judgment call, I folded my arms and leaned back in my chair.

June continued. The man was caring, loving, and supportive. He got to know her family and they treated him as if he was their own. They had a great relationship. They dated for a couple of years. He was always around for her and treated her like a queen. He always paid for their dates. He was always a gentleman in her company. June couldn't have asked for a better man.

She then confessed that she'd treated him like *trash*.

She was mean to him. She did so because he was too nice and sweet. It became too much for her. So she started seeing another man.

The other man treated her like dirt. He dogged her and made her cry. He was not caring or considerate. He rarely paid for their outings and always made her feel like he was doing her a favor. He was completely opposite from the nice, loving man.

I just shook my head. I was ready to lay into her, as her Gay Best Friend, but June went on to reveal a shocker to me. "You know, Terrance, I actually *liked* the treatment I was getting from the new man."

I looked at her like she was crazy.

"His behavior was something I was used to. The way he treated me made me more intrigued with him. He was my bad boy."

Yeah, it was time for me to let loose on her. Ladies do it all the time. You run after the bad boy, the one your mother tells you to stay away from, but you are intrigued, and curious to find out what he's about. Despite the emotional and sometimes physical abuse you endure, you want to make him love you. (I am literally sitting here shaking my head wishing I could reach out and grab you!)

Please know that Spirit is *not* going to send you someone who will hurt you in any way. He will not be verbally, physically or emotionally abusive.

*Love is patient, love is kind. It does not envy, it does not boast, it is not proud. It is not rude, it is not self-seeking. It is not easily angered. It keeps no record of wrongs. Love does not delight in evil but rejoices with the truth. It always protects, always trusts, always hopes, always perseveres* (1 Corinthians 13:4-7).

---

After June confessed her desire for the bad boy, she expressed how she desperately needed to grow spiritually. She needed to break out of the idea that *bad* was good for her.

Well, hell yeah! I am glad she got it, because choosing someone who is not healthy for you will place you in an unhealthy situation, like the hospital or mental ward.

"Consciously, I know that bad is not good for me, but something keeps me intrigued with the bad boy," June continued.

"Look, June," I said, wishing I had a stronger drink than my fruit punch at that moment. "You are a pretty woman. You seem intelligent, and you have some sense. But as your Gay Best Friend, it is my duty to tell you the truth. If you keep running after the bad boy, you are going to end up lonely and unhappy for the rest of your life. Or you may meet a man who will do some serious damage to you."

"Well, here is the thing," June said. "I am in a new relationship with a man I met at church. He reminds me a lot of the good man I dated from my past. That man loved and cared for me. This new guy is very much the same way. He really loves me. I don't want to make the same mistake I did once before."

I sat up in my seat, placed my delicious food on the table, and leaned in close to June. I said to her, "You have to forgive yourself. You accepted a behavior you thought was good for you, and now you know better. Don't beat yourself up over it. You're older, wiser, and smarter now."

I then told June she could either call the man she hurt in her past and ask him for forgiveness, or she could write him a letter. "You are holding on to the guilt and pain you caused him. Once you ask for his forgiveness, it will help you in breaking the cycle and the guilt you are carrying around with you," I said.

By doing this, June could free herself, heal her soul, and allow herself to love the man she was currently with.

Last, I told her to be patient and take it slow. "You need to be honest and up-front with your new man. Let him know where you are emotionally, and that you are working on allowing love to come in your life."

I smiled and held her hand. She gently squeezed my hand. I could tell she appreciated the comfort and someone telling her everything was going to be okay. Honestly, June needed time to heal from all the years of guilt and pain she had been fretting over.

As stubborn a woman as June is (because she loved the bad boy and it was hard to shake him) she smiled and said, "I really am going to take your advice. It's time for a change."

"Girl, you better take my advice. This isn't cheap wisdom."

We both laughed.

Lo and behold, June called me almost a year later. "Guess what?" She said. "I did what you said, and my boyfriend and I are talking about getting married."

Isn't love grand?

And it was all in a gay's day's work.

Ladies, think of the many times you may have brushed a man off because he was too nice or too sweet. Think of the many times you didn't let love come into your life because he did not make enough money, or you didn't like the career he had, or where he lived, or the type of car he drove.

Spirit has brought many men in your life. They have come and gone. Poof! Disappeared. Absent.

I am telling you, you no longer have to let love slip through your fingers and out of your life. Take notice and see if the current man in your life, or the one you need, is caring, loving, focused, a hard worker, family-oriented, and spiritually grounded. If you have that man, or know of him, be open to receiving the gift that Spirit has sent you.

Take a cue from India.Arie's lyrics: sing to yourself, "I am ready for love."

# Chapter 13

# Every Man Is Not Relationship Material: Get Up and Move On!

If a man tells you that he is not interested in a relationship, then he is not the man for you. Honey-cakes, you need to know that every man you meet is not relationship material.

"Well, damn, Terrance, what man *is* relationship material?" You may ask.

He is one who is able to freely communicate his feelings and emotions and not worry about being judged. He is a man who is comfortable showing love and joy to a woman. A man who is able to appreciate a woman and treat her like a queen. A man who can spend time with the guys and still make quality time for his special lady. He enjoys learning new things. He is not afraid to admit when he is wrong and is willing to work on his weaknesses. He is strong enough to take charge, and yet strong enough to let you take charge.

I can see your hands now waving in the air. Oh yes I can. You're screaming, "*Yes, hallelujah!*" You want to know where this man is and why you haven't met him. You were hoping that your current or ex-boyfriend was this type of man.

Guess what a lot of women do if a man is not quite up to her standards? She actually thinks she can *turn him into* that type of man. Many women feel they can change him over time. Can you believe in this day and age, there are women who still think this is possible?

But of course this isn't you, because you don't have the time or energy to be trying to fix anybody up. (You are still working on *you*, remember?)

In my travels across the country, I've met scores of women who think they have found the one. He is their Mr. Right. He has it going on. So I ask them, "Why are you waiting to talk to me? If you have met 'The One,' then you don't need advice from me."

But then they start telling me their stories. I listen, just hoping they are not going to say those words I truly hate to hear women say, "But I love him. I really want to make this work." Or "I think he can change. He just needs someone like me in his life."

Right. Just like you need another hole in your head.

Not all men—even spiritually minded men—are relationship material. A lot of them are still fresh and young on their spiritual walk, so it will take them some time to fully develop the spiritual side of themselves. They are constantly challenged by temptations all around them. They are not quite ready to settle down.

Other men are just not ready for any type of serious commitment with anyone. They are perfectly content being bachelors.

Just like many of you. Some ladies need to be single and work on their spiritual walk. Trying to be in a relationship right now is probably not in those ladies' best interest. There are some things they are still discovering about themselves, and a man will only distract them and take them off their course.

Let's just imagine for a minute that you are confident, very spiritual, and prayerful. You know yourself like the back of your own hand. You are ready to settle down in a relationship. You meet quite a few men, and you can't seem to pick which one you want.

Awww, the joys of having a choice.

I'm going to do you a favor and break it down a little further for some of you. Just in case you still don't know what a man who is not relationship material looks like.

If a man tells you that he is not interested in being in a relationship, then guess what? That means not with *you*, either. I don't care how many times he has taken you out on a date, sexed you really well, and given you late-night conversation. True, his actions are saying something totally different, but if he says he is not interested in a relationship, then he is *not interested*. Let him go. Do not get your hopes up thinking you can change his mind. Because the truth of the matter is, everything he is doing with you, and all the time he may be spending with you, he is doing the same with other women. They are getting equal amounts of his time.

Let him go and move on. It will save you untold time and aggravation trying to figure out why the two of you are not a couple.

If a man tells you that he has a girlfriend but is always looking for more female friends, *run, run, run!* He is not faithful. That is a tell-tale *neon* sign that he will not be faithful to you, either. Some women actually think it's cute to be dating a man with a girlfriend, or many lady friends, and they think they are getting one over on the unsuspecting girlfriend. Trust me, there is nothing cute about it. There is a thing known as karma. You may not feel its effects immediately, but trust me, honey, karma will come back and bite you in the butt. Leave that man and drama alone.

If a man tells you that he just came out of a relationship, ladies, then you'd better believe he is not ready to jump into another relationship immediately. Let him have his time to grieve, mourn, or celebrate his way out of his situation. Trying to get someone to commit to another relationship when they just came out of one is a disaster waiting to happen. But some women will try to convince that man that they are not like the ex-girlfriend who did him wrong. She will not nag him like his ex, and unlike his last girlfriend, she won't require a lot of time and attention.

Lies, pure lies, I tell you.

Think about the amount of time you needed to get over your last serious ex.

If you don't allow him the time to heal and let go of his ex, she will show up in your relationship with him. Trust me.

If a man only calls you after midnight to come over to his house, well, this is an easy one. I shouldn't have to go any further and explain. But just in case you don't understand, Ms. Honey, it's a *booty call*. That's right. He does not see you as a woman he would like to be in a relationship with. He only sees you as a sex partner. If that's what you are looking for, then knock yourself out. If you are looking for a good man who respects you, move on. This one only thinks of you as a sexual being.

If a man is not willing to define the relationship he has with you, then you are not in a relationship. If every time you bring up the subject, his response is "You're cool," "We're just chilling," or "Why we got to define this?" This man is clearly not the one for you. He cannot be honest or open enough to express how he feels for you. Why would you sit around waiting on a little boy? Only small children cannot clearly articulate their feelings. The man for you will not hesitate or clam up when it's time to share his feelings and emotions. He will certainly be able to express if he is into you, and that you are his one and only lady.

If you have been seeing a man for over six months and you've never been to his home, have not met any of his friends or family members, and you are still not sure where he works, this is *surely* a clear indication that you don't have a relationship with him. You know nothing about this man.

Why is he being so discreet? He is obviously hiding something. Let him go and move on. Why would you want to be with a man who is not willing to share his personal life with you? It's not worth it to play detective and explore his background. (And I know some of you will, because you like snooping and being nosy.) If he is not forthright with basic information, just let him and his secrets go. Some things, you are better off not knowing.

I have a good friend who is just like most of you. She's a hopeless romantic. "Jacqueline" and I openly discuss our relationships and the intimate details of our lives with one another. I can call on her for anything, and she can do the same with me. We console one another, tell the truth to each other, and get on one another's last nerve sometimes. Yet, we always work out our differences. I am her Gay Best Friend, and we respect one another.

Each day we have our early morning talks. We can talk for hours about everything. During most of the calls, it's a counseling session. We counsel one another on various things from career to relationships.

For nearly a year, most of the counseling sessions were about Jacqueline and why she couldn't seem to find a man to be in a relationship with. Jacqueline is smart, beautiful, rich, has a successful career, and is extremely loving. She just couldn't put her finger on what the problem was.

Jacqueline works on herself non-stop. She goes to the gym regularly and has a personal trainer. She eats healthily. She goes to church every Sunday and she is spiritually grounded. She even sees a professional therapist who has helped her overcome some of her anxieties and childhood issues.

One thing, however: Jacqueline doesn't have high regard for herself. She's always comparing herself to other women. In looks, status, and career, she rarely focuses on her own great qualities. She is always trying to figure out why other women are in relationships and she isn't.

Every other week for a year, she would meet a new man. She was always sure he was "The One." She would be so excited when we talked, but by the end of the week, her excitement was gone. She was back to her pity party.

The men Jacqueline meets are great guys. They are just not "The One" for her.

Once, she met a police officer who was fun and, according to her, "great in bed," but his schedule was so demanding that they never spent much time together. They never could seem to make their schedules work.

Then there was a man in another state, about three hours away. She met him while he was in town on a business trip. They spent a lovely weekend together, but he never made any other attempts to come visit her. Jacqueline was always flying or driving to see him. Now, as her Gay Best Friend, I finally told her that if he was really interested in being with her, he would find the time, money, and energy to get to come visit her. Jacqueline stopped going to see him and the relationship ended.

Then there was another man she met, one who lived in New York, and they started dating. He was *very* promising. They went out a few times and Jacqueline enjoyed his company. They had great conversations and everything seemed fine. Until she discovered he had a dog. He told Jacqueline he could not spend too much time away from home because he had to care for his dog. Not a problem. She suggested they could spend time at her place. Only that was an issue because he lived in the Bronx and she lived in Brooklyn. He didn't want to leave his dog alone for long periods of time.

So she suggested that she could spend time at his place. When she took him home (because he didn't have a car), he would never invite her in. His excuse was that his house was a mess and he didn't want her to see his house in that manner.

I told Jacqueline that if he was interested in being with her, he would clean his house and find someone to sit for his dog. She got the message and that relationship ended as well.

One day while Jacqueline and I were talking, I heard Spirit speak to me. Spirit told me to tell her, "Every man is not relationship material."

So I told her what Spirit said. She stopped talking and listened.

"Jacqueline, every man you meet doesn't have to be 'The One,'" I said. "Just enjoy being out with him and don't start planning the wedding while you are sitting across from him. When you are out on your first date with a man talking about marriage and children, that is jumping the gun. These are generally not topics of discussion on a first date. A man is not thinking about marriage on his first date with a woman. It can be very intimidating to a man if you start talking about a serious relationship and you just met him."

I told Jacqueline to not appear so desperate. Men can sense when a woman is out for the kill. This energy will send any man running. It also explained why Jacqueline could never get a third date with most of the men.

Ladies, are some of you just like Jacqueline?

Don't act like you are not sizing the man up to see if he is marriage potential. You do it all the time.

Divas, as your Gay Best Friend I am going to be very frank with you. Don't give in so easily to a man. Make sure that your Spirit is on guard, helping you to discern between what you want and what you need. You have to listen to your Spirit and ask God for guidance.

Well, a few days later after my advice to Jacqueline, she told me that she finally got it. She understood what Spirit was saying when I told her that every man is not relationship material. She said that she was going to stop putting so much focus on being in a relationship and instead, she was going to focus on the date and enjoy being out and having fun.

Trust me, I know it can be difficult when you think you have met the man for you and then discover that he's not. It's perfectly okay. You will be fine and you will get over it. The great thing about it is you can take the stress off yourself. I know some of you probably would like to be in an intimate relationship, but take the time to get know yourself first. Explore *you* and the things that bring you joy. Discover the pleasures of life that bring you happiness.

More important, take your time. What are you in such a rush for? There is no need to jump into a relationship with someone and then find out several months later he's not "The One." Take the time to get to know him, and in the process you will get to learn and know yourself.

## Chapter 14

# You Get What You Ask For: Recognize the Difference Between a Winner and a Loser

*Ask, and it shall be given you; seek, and ye shall find;
knock, and it shall be opened unto you:
For every one that asketh receiveth; and he that
seeketh findeth; and to him that knocketh it shall be
opened.*

—Matthew 7:7-8

I guess you can't get it any simpler. It's right there, translated into plain English from the Bible:
*What you ask for shall be given to you.*

Many times when I speak with women, they tell me how hard it is to find a man and the difficulties they have encountered meeting men they feel are worth their time. I simply ask them, have you *asked* for the man you need?

Some genuinely look astonished, because they realize that they have *not* asked for the man they desire. Others tell me that they have asked, but he has not shown up yet.

I usually answer, have you been *specific* in your request?

That's when I usually get the look as if a light bulb has gone off over their heads. Finally!

A lot of women, it turns out, have *not* given any thought to the type of man they need, nor have they verbally or literally asked for him.

They then ask me, "What do you mean?" It's at that moment I know they need a Gay Best Friend.

I ask them to tell me about the man currently in their life or the previous men in their life. They start telling me about the many men who have come and gone. They tell me about the current boyfriend who is not quite worth their time, or how they wish he could change and be or do better.

I simply say, "You got what you asked for."

I tell you, some folks hate hearing the truth. They get indignant. (Don't get mad at me, darling. I didn't choose him, you did.)

There are clearly signs to help recognize when you have a loser:

- He doesn't want to work.
- He borrows money from you.
- He lives at home with his mother, not because he has to, but because he wants to, and he is over twenty-five.
- He has several different baby mothers and never visits his children.
- He smokes weed all day, every day, and plays video games with his boys.
- He drives your car while you are at work and doesn't put gas in it.
- He can't cook, clean, or do any type of household chores.

You get my drift, right? If your current man (or previous boyfriend) has qualities that are of the loser kind, then it's time to do some rethinking, reevaluating, and reassessing in your life.

If you are looking for a winner, then you have to be a winner. Like attracts like.

"What is a winner?" You may ask. Well, he is the complete opposite of a loser.

- He has his own apartment or home, car, money, and career.
- He takes you out to dinner, movies, and cultural events, and wants to travel with you.
- He doesn't ask you for money.

- He's not sitting at home playing video games all day, smoking weed with his boys. He has direction and goals.
- He knows what he wants out of life for himself and the woman in his life.
- He's not sleeping around "because there is nothing else to do."
- He has a relationship with God and attends somebody's church, synagogue, or mosque.
- The respect he gives his mother is the same respect he gives you.

You get my drift. You can identify a winner when you see him.

Now, let's you and I take a brief inventory. Yes, right now! Get a sheet of paper and a pen. I want you to make a list of the qualities your current (or previous) boyfriend has that you love. They are the qualities you adore about him.

Your list should look something like this:

| *Positive Attributes:* |
| --- |
| *Spiritual* |
| *Loves children* |
| *Believes in family and marriage* |
| *God-loving and attends services regularly* |
| *Communicative* |
| *Makes quality time to spend with me* |
| *Considerate of my feelings* |

When you are done with that list, I want you to make another list. This one will include all the qualities that you *don't* like about him. Write down all the things that make your blood boil and your nerves fray.

| *Negative Attributes:* |
| --- |
| *Inconsiderate* |
| *Talks with his mouth full of food* |
| *Bad table manners* |
| *Mama's boy—too dependent on his mother* |
| *Serial cheater* |
| *He is sloppy and messy—his room in his mother's house looks like a tornado hit it* |
| *Still thinks he's in high school/college, just wants to hang with his male friends, and not with me.* |

Observe both lists. Take a close look. A *real* close look. Don't be scared.

Compare them to each other. Now think about everything you've ever said about the type of man you wanted and needed. All the comments and affirmations you said to yourself, and to your girlfriends over bottles of wine. Aren't you amazed to see everything you've ever said is on those lists? They are on both lists—the good and the bad.

If you have more items on the good list, then you are well on your way to getting closer to what you need. If you have more on the other side, well...let's just say that we've got our work cut out for us.

Yes, we, because as your Gay Best Friend, I have to whip you into shape. I have to make sure you get what you want and need. You'll thank me later.

Now let's do another exercise. Let's put together your ideal man. Get another clean sheet of paper and at the top of the page write "THE MAN I NEED." Notice the last word is NEED, not WANT. The wanting of something only creates more wanting of it. You want more clothes, time, a car. The list goes on and on. Scripture states, "The Lord is my shepherd, I shall not want." Also, Scripture states that God will supply all your needs. He will fulfill the desires of your heart. (He doesn't say anything about your wants.)

I *really* want you to distinguish between your needs and your wants. There is a difference, trust me. You need water. You need a home. You need food. You need a job. You need money.

You want a luxury car. You want more clothes. You want a trip. You want, want, want, and want.

Our American culture glorifies luxury goods, huge homes, expensive automobiles, excessive jewelry and extreme wealth. It becomes a race to compete with one another, and it leads to spiritual emptiness.

Check this out. The first line of the Twenty-third Psalms says, *the Lord is my shepherd, I shall not want.* Yet the first thing out of our mouths is so often what we *want*.

Think about it. Do you really *need* more money, or do you *want* more money? Because the truth of the matter is if you could manage the $25,000, $30,000, $40,000, or $75,000 salaried job you have, then the Lord would bless you with even more abundance. But because most folks can't manage their weekly check (you know who you are), how can God bless you with more? Remember: He will never give you more than you can bear.

If you can't manage your finances for yourself, how can you honestly expect to manage or handle another adult in your life? If you can barely manage being lower- to middle-class, then how can you expect to be in a relationship with someone who is upper-middle or upper class? Stay in your lane.

Now I want you to write these categories on the page: Personality, Career, Family, Education, Health, Emotions, and Wealth.

In each of these categories I want you to write what is important to you. For example, next to "Personality"—Is he outgoing? Does he have a sense of humor? Is he a thinker? Does he have an inquisitive nature? Is he laid back?

| *The Man I Need* | |
|---|---|
| *Personality* | |
| *Career* | |
| *Family* | |
| *Education* | |
| *Health* | |
| *Emotions* | |
| *Wealth* | |

Then do the same next to "Education." Does a college education matter to you? Do you need someone who has graduated high school? Or does it matter at all about his educational background?

You get my point.

When you verbally ask or write out your request, you are telling Spirit that you are open to receiving the goodness in store for you. You are speaking your man into existence through language. It's how the world was created. It was spoken into existence. *God said let there be light and there was light* (Genesis 1:3).

When you ask Spirit for the type of man you deserve, you are letting Spirit know that you understand all blessings and gifts come from a source beyond yourself.

When you finish your list, write in big bold letters at the bottom of the page: "AND SO IT IS." This statement is a declaration. You are affirming what is so.

Once you've done this, get another clean sheet of paper. (Stop complaining! I hear you out there, "How many sheets of paper do I need?" The truth is, you need a whole *notebook*, preferably one with more than two hundred pages. You are going to need a lot of paper, because you are going to be ever-increasing your list, changing it, and deleting things.)

With this sheet of paper you are writing your "I AM" list. This is your statement of who you are. Yes, I know you are probably thinking, "I already know me. What do I need to do a list about me for?"

Honestly, do you really know yourself? I mean really know who you are? Just as I figured.

| *I AM: Positive Attributes:* |
| --- |
|  |
|  |
|  |
|  |

| *I AM: Negative Attributes:* |
| --- |
|  |
|  |
|  |
|  |

In each of the categories you did for the man you are seeking, I need for you to list all your qualities, both good and bad. And be honest with yourself!

Not that I don't believe you will be honest enough with yourself, but I want you to call your friends and ask *them* to tell you about yourself. Why? Because they will be honest with you and tell you the truth. If they are anything like me, your Gay Best Friend, they will be *brutally* honest.

After compiling your lists of positives and negatives, observe the things on the negative list. These are things you need to work on. Your behaviors and attitudes that need adjusting. You've got to be willing to look at those things as ways of building a better you. You are a work in progress. Your positive attributes will always be played up to the fullest, but the negatives are often heard loudly and clearly, even though you may feel you are concealing them. Or you may think they are minor, but they are not.

Take all your lists and put them someplace where you can occasionally look at them—I suggest every week or month. It depends on what's on your lists. If you have more negatives, then I strongly suggest checking every week.

These lists are your guide. You can adjust, change, or add to them at any time. Because the truth of the matter is, that you (and other people) do change.

I also need for you to understand that *you* are responsible for all the men you have invited into your life for relationships. Yes, *all* the men. Even those you wish you never had met. (Trust me, we all have some fools we wish we'd never met.)

Whatever you believe in your heart, your life will bring the experience into fruition. When you speak of no good men, men who are dogs, or men who are emotionally unavailable, that is exactly what you will attract. You've heard the saying, *Be careful what you ask for because you just might get it.*

Put another way, *But even now I know that God will give you whatever you ask* (John 11:22).

Imagine if you frequently spoke of love, joy, peace, and a good man. Imagine if you spoke of a man who is kind, considerate, and understanding. Imagine what you could bring into your life if you spoke of the goodness associated with a man you desired.

Let me tell you about a friend of mine, an R&B singer who lives in New York, who was always down and out because she could not seem to find the man she wanted. "April" would call me every day with the same complaint. She couldn't seem to find a man. Everyone else seemed to be able to get a man and be in relationships, why not her? She was successful, glamorous, and, hell, she was a star!

I would always tell her to be patient and her man would come. I also reminded April that maybe this was not the time for her to be in a relationship, but to focus on loving herself and doing other things that made her happy, like a hobby or something else to keep her preoccupied. *Anything* other than the thought of a man.

You know what? That is a good idea for everybody, not just April. For all you single women out there sitting around waiting on a man, get a hobby. It is a great idea to keep your mind occupied and fulfilled. A hobby gives a sense of accomplishment. And this way, you don't have to dwell on the sadness or emptiness in your life.

You can join a reading group, teach a class at your local community center, or take a class at the local college or university. Just don't sit around moping.

But I know a lot of ladies are guilty of sitting around discussing men all the time with their girlfriends. And every time they watch a nighttime television drama or a reality show that deals with finding romance, it reminds them that they are alone. When they are out running errands and see all the couples, they begin to daydream and wonder if it's ever going to happen for them.

It will happen.

But just like my friend April, women who so desperately want to be in a relationship never hear any of my advice or suggestions. Well, let's just say that April heard them, but it wasn't what she wanted to hear.

We sometimes hear only what we want to hear. If someone is not playing into our pity party, then we keep whining and whining until they agree. (Unlike me. I just get off the phone. "I got to go." Click!)

So one day I finally told April to sit down and write out the type of man she felt she needed. I told her to describe him in detail. How did he look, what type of personality did he have, and most important, how would he treat her?

April was excited to do this exercise because it was something she had never thought to do. She immediately started the process.

April would call me every other day to let me know of her progress and how much fun she was having. I urged her to keep going and to let me know when she was finished with her list.

By the end of the week April was done, and boy, was she *excited*. I told her that she had learned to ask Spirit for what she needed in her life. Spirit would oblige her with what she asked for because she was deserving and loving.

Lo and behold, April called me two months later with the news she had met a man, "Carl." She was so excited. He was everything on her list. He was gorgeous, tall, funny, caring, communicative, and churchgoing. April was bubbling with joy. She could not believe the man she asked for had shown up in her life.

Then a few weeks later, she called to tell me there was a snag in her list. The man she was so excited about did not have a job. Carl was between jobs and living at home with his family.

My friend April is a millionaire, owns her own home, and performs all over the world. She grew up in an upper-middle-class family in the suburbs. Carl grew up in the housing projects. He was from the 'hood in Brooklyn. There is nothing wrong with that. I know many people who come from different backgrounds and get together. So I couldn't understand her problem, but I had a feeling I knew where it was coming from.

Carl liked Popeyes chicken and drinking forty-ounce beers. April enjoys Café on Park Avenue and drinking red wine. I have never seen her go into a fast-food restaurant and order something. I have never seen forty-ounce beers, Kool-Aid, or soda in April's refrigerator. I rarely see junk food in her house. Still, I wondered what the problem could be. They just have different tastes.

I asked her, "So what's wrong? Did you put on your list that the man you wanted had a job?" She replied no.

"I just assumed he would," she said.

I then asked, "Did you ask for a man who came from the same type of background and upbringing as yourself?" Again, she replied no.

"You got exactly what you asked for. Why are you complaining?"

As much time as April had spent on her list, she'd left off a few key things that she assumed were natural. Her focus was more on his looks and health. She told me, "Boy, I wanted a fine tall dark man with a muscular body. I didn't spend too much time on career, emotional well-being, and education. At the time I was making my list, those things were not important to me."

"Well, since they were not important to you, you got what you got," I said. "You can start over and create a new list. This time, be more specific."

Ladies, take a moment and think about the type of men you have encountered in your life. Are these the type of men you have been speaking into existence? Are these the type of men you've asked for, but forgot that's what you said out loud?

Most times when we keep encountering the same type of person in relationships, it's generally because we keep telling the universe that is what we need. When you learn to be more specific and ask for what you need from Spirit, there is no doubt that your request will be heard and answered.

Take the time to review the lists you've created. Look at each category and everything you wrote under them. Focus on the areas you feel are more important to you. It's okay if some things simply do not matter to you. Feel free to add more categories if you desire.

Once you have completed your list, go over it again to see if there is anything missing or something you should add. If you are satisfied with your list, put it someplace safe.

Now, look at the list you've created about yourself. Are you everything you say that you are on the list? Are you ready for the man you asked for to show up?

If yes, then, get ready, because Spirit will honor your request.

# Chapter 15

# Listen:
# It Will Save You a World of Headaches

*Listen, my child, and accept my words, so that the years of your life will be many. I will guide you in the way of wisdom and I will lead you in upright paths.*
—Proverbs 4:10-11.

When people show you who they are, believe them. When people tell you who they are, listen. When a *man* tells you who he is, listen.

One of the biggest pitfalls for women is the inability to listen. (Actually, it's not just women who do not listen; people *in general* do not listen.)

As a man, I can tell you after conducting workshops and groups with men across the country, one of the main reasons men leave their relationships is because the women didn't listen to them. That was unanimously agreed upon by all the men.

Listening requires you to intently pay undivided attention to others as they are speaking to you and be present in the moment.

It's the same when Spirit speaks to you. You have to be open and willing to listen when Spirits provides you with guidance, direction, and answers. Spirit cannot speak with you if you are busy running around, inundating yourself with e-mails, the phone, the computer, the television, the radio, and other everyday activities. When Spirit speaks, you'd better pay attention. Take the time to be still, quiet yourself, and listen as Spirit provides you with everything you need.

One key to attracting a man is listening to him. My gosh, that is a wonderful attribute to have. Just to sit, be quiet, and *listen* to him when he speaks with you.

When you are attentive when you meet a man, you can hear him when he tells you that he beat his last girlfriend. You can hear when a man tells you that he is not interested in a relationship at this time. You can hear when he tells you that his favorite meal is fried chicken, macaroni and cheese, and collard greens. Then you will not be trying to turn his favorite meal into chicken cordon bleu, spinach, and carrots. (Not that there is anything wrong with those foods, but, my darling, when you listen to him, you will know what his favorite foods really are).

Then again, people hear what they want to hear.

The reason most women don't listen is that they are listening through a filter of their own feelings, perceptions, and thoughts.

For example, when you see a man you are attracted to, your listening is focused on the way he looks and the way he is dressed. You are typically more interested in his appearance than to what he is saying.

Picture two men on the street—one in a well-tailored suit with a briefcase (well-groomed, manicured, and professional-looking), the other wearing Timberland boots, an oversized T-shirt, a baseball cap, and baggy jeans. Both men are in their thirties and very attractive, with similar educational backgrounds. But one man is looking for a job, while the other is an executive in the entertainment industry.

If both men approached you respectfully and courteously at different times during the day, to which man would you give your attention? Which man would you most listen to? You would probably listen more intently to the man in the baggy jeans, over-sized T-shirt, baseball cap, and Timberland boots. "Why?" You ask.

Because you will probably be listening to find something *wrong* with him. You will pay more attention to him because you are judging his appearance. You have a preconceived idea about men dressed in that manner, and you are listening to see if he falls into one of the categories you think he fits. He probably doesn't have a job, you may think. He has several different baby mommas, each with several children. He lives at home with his mother. He doesn't have a car.

Ugh!

By the way, I used this example to show you that you can't judge a book by its cover. The man in the well-tailored suit and briefcase is, of course, the jobless one. *He* lives at home with his mother. *He* has two different baby mommas, and if it was up to him, he wouldn't pay child support.

The other brother with the Timberland boots, baggy jeans, fitted baseball cap, and oversized T-shirt? He's the entertainment executive.

Let me tell you something, precious. Listening happens with your ears, not your eyes. You will miss out on some important information if you keep judging a man by his cover, rather than the contents.

Listen with your ears, and you will hear him when he says, "I am not looking for anything serious." When a man tells you this, RUN! Run fast. Far, far into the hills. Get away. Don't think you can change him or his mind. You can't. You won't. You will fail. Abort the mission. You could be a saint sent directly from Heaven, but he has already told you his truth. "I am not looking for anything serious." Refuse to listen, and you will find yourself crying all alone, wondering why he can't see you for the wholesome, wonderful, and good woman you are.

It's not you. It's him.

I also understand when a man wants to end a relationship and says, "It's not you, it's me." It's often a shocker to hear, especially when you didn't see it coming. You've been the doting girlfriend and suddenly he tells you it's over because he needs some space and time. You're confused, angry, and hurt all at the same time. You need answers. Is it you? Is there someone else? What can you do to fix it?

Girl, I have *been* there.

I don't understand women who throw tantrums and fight with a man because he wants to leave them. Cursing, spitting, and acting unladylike. What is that about? Why fight to be with someone who clearly doesn't want to be in a relationship with you?

When he wants to walk away, *let him*.

I know it sounds hard to do, but trust me, as your Gay Best Friend, if a man wants to leave, you need to *let him go*. Once a man has made up his mind to leave a relationship, he has already done it. Sometimes months before. During those months, he was mentally preparing himself for the conversation and backlash. He was also trying to figure out the right time and moment to have that conversation. So no amount of talking, fighting, arguing, or crying will get him to change his mind. Mentally and emotionally, he has *already left the relationship*.

Sure, you can talk it out with him to find out what happened, but be prepared to hear answers you may not like. Just listen. Take it in. And when he is done, hold your head up, thank him for the lesson, wish him well on his journey, swing your long luxurious weave in the wind, and walk elegantly out the door.

Oh, trust me, his jaw will drop. Then you can call me up, your Gay Best Friend, so we can go get us a good drink and laugh about the knucklehead and his "finding-myself" speech.

I got an e-mail from "Samantha" in Chicago a while back. She was seeking advice about what to do for her boyfriend, "Greg," for Christmas. They had dated a while back and ended their relationship after a few years. They had since reconnected and been back together for a little over a year. Samantha and Greg were giving it a second chance because they figured since their time apart, they had matured and grown spiritually.

Samantha said she wanted to do something nice for Greg. They had not been on a trip together, so she wanted to plan a nice weekend away to a tropical island. She wanted to go someplace romantic and quiet where they could spend some quality time together. Besides, she just wanted to get out of the city.

Samantha's dilemma was that Greg did not want to go on a romantic trip to a tropical island. He did not want to go anywhere, for that matter. When she asked him what he wanted for Christmas, Greg's answer was that he simply wanted a PlayStation gaming console.

Samantha, being presumptuous, had already started gathering brochures, getting prices, and searching locations for the perfect trip. She was upset because Greg was not interested in participating in planning the perfect getaway for the two of them.

Samantha wanted to know what to do. She wanted him to be just as excited as she was about the romantic trip that she was planning. Instead of sending her a long drawn out e-mail (I was busy sipping on my cocktail, marinating on my own relationship), I simply responded with, "Stop planning the trip and buy him the PlayStation."

Within minutes—no, make that seconds—Samantha responded with another lengthy e-mail filled with all the *whys, buts, ifs,* and *how-comes.* She had put a lot of time and effort into planning this romantic trip, and she did not want to give up on it just yet.

I set my cocktail to the side and dutifully responded as her Gay Best Friend.

"Samantha, thank goodness I am not in Chicago right now, because you wouldn't like to see my face and feel my wrath in person. So, I am going to be gentle with you. You obviously are committed to doing what *you* want to do and not listening to your boyfriend, Greg, nor listening to me, your Gay Best Friend.

"Now, if you want to make your relationship work (and not have a boyfriend on a trip with you whom I can *guarantee* will not enjoy it as much as you will), then buy him the PlayStation and please, listen to him."

Don't get me wrong, I understood that she wanted to go away on a romantic trip and spend time with her boyfriend, but this was not the time to do it. I told her to buy the PlayStation and in a few months, while he was excitedly playing his video games, she could bring up the trip. If she did that, I told her, I was sure Greg would be more than excited to go, because she would have listened to him the first time. He would greatly appreciate that she did not force the trip on him and would probably be ready to join in on the planning of the trip down the road.

A few months later, I got an e-mail from Samantha.

From the Bahamas.

She thanked me profusely for recommending that she get Greg the PlayStation. What she got in return was a happy, fun, and sexy vacation in the Bahamas with her man.

You get my point, right? Listening to your mate will make things *much* easier and happier in the long run. If you stop trying to get things done *your* way and learn to work together, you will not spend so much time arguing over things, getting bent out of shape and frustrated.

I'm not saying you have to always give in to him. I am simply implying that you should listen to each other. You hear him, and let him hear you. If you connect with him where he is speaking from, in his heart and mind, your relationship will be filled with joy, peace, happiness, and love.

Now, about another thing.

It amazes me when couples are arguing and suddenly, out of the blue, a woman will bring up something that happened last week, last month, or last year.

It seems to men, sometimes, that women hold things bottled up inside all that time, bubbling and brewing, just waiting to lay into us and let us have it.

You could be arguing over why he didn't pick you up from work on time, and from out of left field, you will bring up last week's incident when he hung out with his boys instead of taking you to the movies like he promised. The two have nothing to do with each other, but you will bring it up. As a matter of fact, you will bring up *everything.*

That's when we as men will look at you like you're crazy and say, "What are you talking about? What does that have to do with this?"

Because people are human, when they argue everybody wants to be right. Instead of listening to one another, they scream and yell at each other trying to score points. And because this is the opportunity you've been waiting for to bring up everything you've allowed to fester, your argument will make you appear as if you've never listened and probably never will. If you'd simply addressed the issue, come to a conclusion, and moved on, then you wouldn't be wasting time and energy trying to reconcile something that happened days, months, or even years ago.

Listen, girl. Listen, process, evaluate, and discuss. Work out the situation and move on. Let it go and don't bring it up. Why hold on to it and let it fester? What good is that to you, or your relationship? You are the catalyst for the type of relationship you desire to have. You have the power to create and build the love you desire. It's all within you. It's all yours. Don't let miscommunication and the inability to listen be the detriment to your relationship.

I met "Carol" at a book signing in South Carolina. An attractive woman with a beautiful smile, Carol approached me afterward and asked if my book *Reclaim Your Power!* would be a great gift for a man who was new to spirituality. She was looking for a way to help him see that she was a good woman for him.

I gave Carol a once-over. She was stunningly dressed, so I gave her a nod of approval, and then I asked what she meant, "Would my book would help this man see if she was a good woman for him?"

She proceeded to tell me about "John," whom she had met at church. They had been seeing one another for the past six months. He was everything she wanted and had asked for.

Carol told me that she'd prayed and asked for a man like John. However, there was one catch. John had been married previously and said he was not ready to settle down with another woman just yet. He was only interested in a friendship with Carol, and he wanted to take things slow. He had a daughter, so he wanted to spend a lot of quality time with her and not introduce any new women in his life. He also had recently moved into an apartment and was taking on a new job.

John said he was in a transition period and was not focused on a relationship.

You should have seen my face. I rolled my eyes and sucked my teeth. I've heard this story a thousand times before. I shook my head.

And before I could say anything. Carol said, "What? You don't understand. I am a good woman and he just needs some time."

I jerked my head back. "No, I *do* understand. You may be a good woman, but you are not the woman for him. He is not interested in being in a relationship right now."

But Carol was convinced that this was the man for her because, as she'd said, *she had prayed and asked for someone like him*. Besides, they got along well and they did spend a lot of time together.

I did another once-over of Carol. It was then I realized she was a dressed-up mess. She wasn't listening to Spirit. If she had been, she would have heard Spirit respond to her prayers, and obviously she hadn't gotten an answer. I am certain Spirit had *not* told her to pursue this man, because clearly he was not available. Carol was instead following *her feelings*. She *felt* that John was the man for her.

If she'd been listening, then she would have *heard* John when he said repeatedly that he was not interested in a relationship, and he had recently come out of a divorce. I was certain John was not looking to jump into something serious so soon.

But sometimes, when a woman wants something, she will be relentless, especially if it's a man she wants. I have seen it too many times.

Carol was determined to make this man see that she was the woman for him. Instead of listening to him, she was caught up in her own idea that they were going to have a relationship. She was on a mission to get John.

Why is it that when someone tells you he is not interested in being in a relationship, it makes him more appealing? There is nothing cute or sexy about pursuing someone relentlessly, especially after he disses you or says something that hurts your feelings and you get all upset.

Girl, go sit down somewhere!

Persistence is not attractive when it becomes insistent, pushy, and aggravating. I am sure that many of you have found it annoying when a man keeps calling, begging, and throwing himself at you.

Let me tell you something. Desperation, loneliness, and fear prevent you from listening. I know you are probably sitting there saying you are not any of these. But somewhere, a woman is reading this book, and she wants to throw it at the wall right now. How *dare* someone call her lonely, desperate, or fearful? (Darling, denial is the first human response.)

I wish someone would explain to me why the most common complaint men have is that women don't listen. (Of course, you may point out, men don't listen either. Which is a very true statement that I will not dispute.)

Yet, I believe I do understand. If you examine your previous or current relationship, I am sure you can find moments when you ignored something important he said. You brushed it off, didn't take it seriously. But for him, it was very serious. He didn't say it to be taken lightly. And yet, you ignored him.

Tsk. Tsk. Tsk.

Reflection is something, isn't it?

Listen up, Ms. Thang.

If you really want to get and keep the man—the spiritual man for you—you need to listen to him. If he tells you that he enjoys watching football all day on Sunday, don't make plans with him that day. Take that afternoon to do something for yourself. If you told a man that on Tuesday nights you spend time with your mother or girlfriends, you would not appreciate him making Tuesday plans with you when he knew this in advance.

If you are looking to be in a relationship and a man says he does not want a relationship, he is *not the man for you.*

So many women tell me that she is going to get the man, and he will love her because she is different. Do you know how many women say this? Do you realize that men hear this all the time?

Sure, you may be different. We are all unique. But if a man is not interested in being a relationship, leave him alone! Forcing someone (or being slick and savvy) will only lead you down a destructive path. And yet, afterward, a lot of women end up disappointed and upset when it doesn't work out.

Listen to men. Listen to Spirit. Spirit is not going to guide you down the wrong path.

In Yolanda Adams' song "Open My Heart," she makes a plea for God to speak to her. She needs desperately to hear a word. If you notice, she stops, gets still, and opens her heart. If you take heed to Yolanda in her heartfelt plea, you will understand that Spirit will provide you with everything you need if you take the time to be still, be quiet, and simply listen.

It is the same with a man.

Listen to what he is expressing and how he is expressing it.

You will have a great and loving relationship once you learn to listen.

# Chapter 16

# Date: It's That Thing You Do Before Sex

The great thing about finding the man for you is that you get the chance to date. The opportunity to have fun, enjoy his company, and most important, keep your options open. If you want to find the man for you, you've got to get in the game and play.

I sometimes think dating is a thing of the past. I rarely hear of men and women going out on dates today. I rarely see couples out on the town having fun. Dating has been dropped in favor of, "If you are the one right now, let's be in a relationship." You meet someone, sleep with him, and tomorrow you are in a relationship. There is no courtship, no taking it slow, no playing the field anymore.

What is going on with women? You let men hold the cards and not court you. That is *so* not fabulous. It is definitely not ladylike, and no Diva would give herself so easily, so readily to a man.

I think because we live in a "got to have it now" society, we no longer have the time or patience to date. We crave instant gratification. So when some women meet a man, they are immediately sizing him up to be their husband instead of someone to date and have fun with.

As we get older, our social and intimate circles get smaller. Remember when you were in high school or in college? You had a plethora of people to choose from to date. Remember when you were younger and could spend hours on the phone? Then you would go out on dates and have fun.

Now that you've gotten older, the long hours on the phone are nonexistent. The dates are no longer fun, but interviews. The dating process is a job, not something joyous and fun.

---

Today, many people resort to the Internet to find a mate. They post their pictures, some general basic information about what they are looking for, and (if they are truthful) their age.

I strongly encourage and suggest stepping out of your comfort zone and be personable and approachable. Get together with a group of friends and visit new parts of the city. Doing different things out of your environment tends to expand your horizons.

I *like* being out in public meeting new and exciting people. Interaction with people is sometimes priceless. I know it does take a certain type of person to be outgoing and bold, and that not everyone is cut out to be adventurous or personable. (Besides, I live in Los Angeles, and there are advantages to living in a major city. There are many places and opportunities to venture to meet new people all the time.)

I want you to go out, anywhere, and *smile*. Speak when others speak to you. Engage in conversations with others. There is nothing like a woman with a bright smile on her face. She has everyone around her laughing and engaged in what she is saying. Put on a sincere smile, and everyone will want to be around you. You will have men falling all over themselves to be next to you, asking to take you out, wanting to wine and dine you. Pumpkin, the dates will be *endless.*

And keep in mind that it's just that, a date. It's not a marriage proposal. It's not an interview session for a potential husband. It is simply a *date.* When a man is out with a woman, he is not sizing her up to see if she is going to be his wife. He is not planning a wedding or wondering how many children he wants to have with her. No! He is on a date and he is out to have fun. If you can get your mind around that, then you will understand how men think and what they are thinking. You will have fun on dates and not be bothered and wondering whether he is sizing you up to meet his mother. (Truly, Ms. Thing, that is the furthest thing from his mind.)

Dating is *going out* to various places in your city. It is an opportunity to experience things you've always wanted to but didn't want to do alone, and now you're in the company of a man (hopefully a fun and outgoing man) who will enjoy the experience with you. If you have a good time with him the first time, *then* you can decide to go out with him again.

Remember, *you* hold the cards. It's your party and he is a guest. You've invited him to be a part of your celebration.

And ladies, ladies, ladies. Stop jumping in bed with these men so soon. I mean, really. Must you hop in the bed just because he took you to a nice restaurant and a nice walk in the park? That is what he is *supposed* to do. He is courting you. He is going to do everything to be close and intimate with you.

Don't make it so easy.

Don't answer the phone every time he calls.

Let him leave messages.

Let him think you are busy and not anxious or desperate and waiting on his call. Return his call later. Give it an hour or two. If you really *are* busy, call him later that evening. I know you really like him and you want to speak to him and hear his voice, but keep in mind he wants to speak with you and hear your voice as well. A good man will wait on your return call.

He has got to win your heart. And your heart is a precious commodity. It isn't just for every man that comes along. The man for you makes you *swoon*. His voice is like music to your ears. His touch is gentle and sends shivers through you. Yes, *that* man. When he walks into a room, you smile and he smiles, because you're equally glad to see one another. He can't wait to see you, and you can't wait to see him. Let him send you flowers and cards (yes, ladies, that is part of courting). You get to find out how romantic he really is. If he is creative and imaginative, he will do things that will have you shaking your head in wonderment.

That is dating.

That is courtship.

That is a man who is willing to work, with much pleasure, to make you his woman—his one and only lady.

I met a woman in Atlanta, "Donna." She was extremely nice and very funny. She told me that she had two young boys, and her dating life was null and void. She was a working mother, so she did not have the time for dating, and she was not going to bring different men around her sons.

Donna had not been out on a date with a man in more than four years.

I don't think y'all really read that.

It had been *four years* since Donna had been on a date. (And some of you think *your* dating life is in the toilet.)

Donna knew what type of man she wanted to be with, but didn't know how or where to find him. "I want to go out on a date, but I wouldn't know where to go," Donna said. "Besides, I am so busy with my boys, I don't think I have time."

"Do you really want to find a man?" I asked Donna.

"Yes," she replied.

I said, "If you want to date, then you have to get a babysitter for your boys, get out of the house, attend social events, and have fun. You are not going to find a man sitting at home every night with your boys."

Now, ladies, I *do* understand that Donna is a working mother with two young boys, but she is still entitled to a life of her own. If Donna waits until her boys are old enough and out of the house, her new excuse will be that she is too old to date. And if *that* is not the excuse, she will find another one. Like Donna, many women find an excuse for not dating.

I hear women often complain that they want to go out but they spend their nights at home. Honey, if you are looking to date or meet a man, he is not going to find you while you are sitting in your house watching *CSI: Miami* or *American Idol.*

Girl, you've got to get out. And please, please be approachable. I have been to so many gatherings where women are sitting around with attitudes or with frowns on their faces. Leave the drama, anger, bitterness, and attitude at home. A man will *definitely* not approach you if you are sitting there pouting with your drink in front of you.

A few weeks later, I heard from Donna. She told me that it had been hard for her at first to get out of the house. She was so used to being at home on the weekends with her boys, it just didn't feel right leaving them. She said she'd thought about what I said, however, and she forced herself to get out there. She called up her girlfriends, and they went to an event sponsored by her sorority. And there were plenty of men there.

But what was even more interesting is that her sons *encouraged* her to go out. They *wanted* to see their mother happy. They *wanted* her to go out and date.

"Terrance, they practically pushed me out the door," Donna wrote.

Can you believe it? For four years Donna had been sitting at home with her sons every night and weekend, and all that time, they actually wanted her to go out and have fun. Donna thanked me again and again. She was much happier and was enjoying her life for the first time.

Here is something I recommend to every person, man or woman. Set up a date with Spirit. Spirit loves when you pay attention to it. It is the time when you are most centered, present, and quiet.

Designate nights or days when you will spend quality time with your spiritual self. When you make an effort to spend time with Spirit, you will also clear space to make time to date a man.

A date with Spirit could be a day at the spa getting pampered. You could spend the day shopping, eating at your favorite restaurant, or curled up in your bed with candles and a good book. Throw on your favorite CD and let it play. Whatever soothes you and makes you feel good, spend time doing it with Spirit.

I also call it "acting as if…"

You've got to *act as if* the man you want to date is already in your life. Don't put your life on hold and stop living just because you have no one to do it with. If you can enjoy being with your spiritual self, you can enjoy being with a man. Don't make the things you enjoy be contingent upon whom you're sharing it with.

To act as if the man you want is already in your life, think about the things you would like to do. Then do them. So when the man does show up, you and he can enjoy them together. He will immediately see how much fun you are because you have been doing it all along.

# Chapter 17

# Let Go of Being Right:
# Don't Make Him Wrong...Right?

Too many times, I have seen women in relationships who are always right. They know the answers to everything. I've seen it in my own family and among friends. No matter what the situation is, these women are right. Especially when it comes to their men—they always know what's best for him.

If a man is in a relationship with a woman who is always telling him how wrong he is and nothing he does is right, he will eventually leave her. There is no doubt about it.

I have heard many men share their horror stories. (OK, they were not precisely horror stories, but they sometimes sound like it.) In my Men's Empowerment, Inc. organization, many men have shared how annoying and nerve-wracking it is for their women to constantly nag and tell them how wrong they are. Men *will* and *do* end their relationships because their women have an undying need to be right.

Girl, don't sit there like you don't know who or what I am talking about.

You know exactly who I am referring to.

I'm talking about the woman who goes off, pointing and waving her finger, rolling her neck and head with her other hand on her hip. Yes, she is on a roll, because her man can never seem to do anything right. Guess what we as men do in that situation? We agree, purely for the sake of not wanting to argue. Now, *some* men will go toe-to-toe with you, but more often than not, we will agree just so you will shut up.

Listen up, ladies. Sometimes you *may* be right, and sometimes you may know what you are talking about. But when you are in a relationship with a man and you are constantly pointing out his faults, you are doing an excellent job of getting rid of him. He will walk right out of your life and leave you to complain all by yourself.

Some of you may be saying, "Good riddance. I don't need a wimpy man. I need a man who will step right up and fight with me. I need a man who can challenge me and go toe-to-toe in a debate."

Don't you realize how draining that is? Constant arguing is unnecessary and causes stress in a relationship. A man does not want to go into an all-out battle with his woman every time they disagree on something. A man is not looking for a woman who is going to berate him and keep going on and on and on about how right she is.

How does it feel when someone is constantly telling *you* how wrong you are? How do *you* feel when your boss or colleagues are always telling you how right they are? Better yet, what about your parents, who know way more than you, and are always reminding you of that fact? It's not a good feeling, is it? After a while, all that negativity can damage a person's self-esteem.

Do you know how many young people grow up with low self-esteem because someone always told them how wrong they were? Many of these young people rebel and become career criminals, drug users, and abusers. They seek out unhealthy relationships and are destructive with their lives.

It is hard for Spirit to communicate with someone who is always right. Spirit can only provide guidance to someone who is willing to listen. If you are never wrong when Spirit is trying to guide you, you will battle over what is the right choice. You will start asking, "Why should I do this? Why is this the right way? I'm going to keep doing it *my* way because I know what the outcome will be. I know what's best for me."

Girl, if that is you, I urge you to get a grip. That is why you are in a mess in the first place.

If you know so well what's best for you, then can you explain why your life is in the rut it's in? Can you explain why, when you are doing it your way and you keep getting the same results, you keep ending up at the same place? You know what they call that? Crazy. Doing the same thing over and over again expecting different results. It's crazy.

But some people may like the results they are getting. They may like the comfort it provides. There is absolutely nothing wrong with that.

If, however, you are looking to live your greatest life, with a wonderful relationship with a powerful man, then you need to stop being right all the time, and stop making him wrong.

A good friend of mine, "Jason," was in a relationship with "Amber," a very intelligent woman who had it going on. She was a leader at her job and in her community. She sat on boards and ran groups. You couldn't find a better woman. She was a take-charge type of woman.

I have always known Jason to like assertive women, but not *aggressive* women. "I like a woman who can stand up for herself and not take no for an answer," Jason told me. "Yet there are some times when she needs to know it's best to let some things go. The best thing to do is to walk away."

I agreed with Jason; that is a great quality for a person to have. If it isn't working, and it's not in your best interest, then walk away.

Anyway, Amber was quite the keeper of wrongs. If Jason did something wrong, she was always quick to point it out and harp on it. At first, Jason wasn't too bothered by this tendency. They would argue and then finally he would say, "Whatever," and move on. But not Amber. She kept tab of all of Jason's wrongs.

How did he know?

Well, Jason told me that one day, while they were arguing, Amber ran into their room and grabbed a pad she kept in her drawer.

"Terrance, she whipped that pad out and immediately gave me the rundown of all the things I had *ever done* she felt were wrong.

She even had the date, time, and direct quotes of my words during the incidents in question."

I sat there looking at Jason, dumbfounded.

Had he just said what I thought he'd said?

As I was wrapping my head around his words, Jason had the same expression on his face that I had. "When she whipped out that notepad, I was in shock," Jason said.

"I couldn't believe that someone would actually keep a *tally* of my wrongs. I thought it was silly, childish, and immature. Why would this smart, intelligent woman keep a record of my wrongdoings?"

"Well, you answered your own question," I said. "Only someone silly, childish, and immature would keep a record of your wrongdoings. What did you do after she pulled out the pad?"

I was on the edge of my seat. I wanted to know more.

"Well, I asked her if she kept a tally of everything I did right, since she was so eager to point out my faults," Jason said.

"What did she say?" I asked.

"She said no," Jason said. "I asked her why not, and she didn't have an answer."

"I figured that," I said.

"But Terrance, instead of getting into an argument with her, I proceeded to tell her of all the great things we've done together. I reminded her of what I've done for her, and all the moments when, instead of arguing with her, I'd simply let it go because she felt the need to be right. I told her that I was not going to sit around arguing with her. I was putting an end to my having to prove to her I was right, or that I'd done nothing wrong. I told her if she wanted to focus on all my negative traits, then she should go right ahead, but I refused to stand there and take it."

"I am so proud of you, Jason," I said.

I really wanted to find Amber and slap some sense into her. She obviously had a good man, but didn't know how to treat him. If she had a Gay Best Friend she wouldn't be acting like she was.

"I finally told Amber that despite all the things she's said and done that were wrong, I never once pointed them out," Jason continued. "As a matter of fact, I've always encouraged her and was her biggest fan."

WOW! Jason deserves a standing ovation. He is the type of man who will stand by you and not just walk out. He will be there in the good times and the bad.

Thank goodness for the Jasons in the world.

But what's obvious to me is that women like Amber have unresolved issues they need to work on. Someone in their past was probably their harshest critic. Someone made them feel less than adequate. It could have been a parent, sibling, teacher, or friend. To cover up their own faults, these women seek out the inadequacies in others. It takes the attention off of themselves.

I mean, there *must* be a reason why they feel the need to be right all the time. It gives them *something* in return. It could be power, control, or a sense of self-righteousness. Imagine the high they must get, knowing they are always right. It must be euphoric. Whatever it is, they are benefiting.

It must be a lonely life to always be right about everything. It must be really heartbreaking to have relationships end because no one wants to be around you.

Think of the family members, friendships, and intimate relationships people like this have lost. Ponder for a moment of the love, joy, and happiness they have missed out on because of their need to be right. Think of what it's costing them.

What if that woman is you?

Yes, you, reading this book.

Imagine what could happen if could you let go of being right. Let go of having to know it all. Simply surrender and let it all go. Make a conscious choice to *let it go*.

There is simply no need to remind someone what they did wrong all the time. Sometimes people have to go off and make mistakes and discover the consequences for themselves. People do not need to hear "I told you so; I was right" all the time. In making mistakes, they will learn their own life lessons. They do not need you to point them out.

My grandmother was a lovely and wise woman. It took a lot to get her angry. I only saw her yell three times while I was growing up. Other than that, she never raised her voice or spoke harshly about anyone.

Now, as I've mentioned, my grandmother raised me since I was a little boy. I watched her endure a lot of emotional highs and lows. Dysfunction is synonymous with my family. My grandmother worked, took care of the household, me, and my grandfather, and never once complained.

I was a very good child. I learned how to be independent and make my own choices. I had to, because my grandmother and grandfather both worked. I learned a lot about independence growing up.

As a matter of fact, I had *too much* freedom. I had very little supervision from adults, which led me to being mischievous at times. You know the saying: Idle hands are the devil's playground.

Because I was such a good boy and well-mannered, I could generally get away with a lot of things. No one ever suspected me. If there was a group of us doing dirt, guess which one of us could *not* have been involved? You guessed it, your Gay Best Friend. I couldn't have been involved, because I was the Goody Two-shoes.

As I got older, I started getting involved with things I had no business messing with. I was getting too big for my britches, and a lot of things started to catch up with me.

My grandmother wouldn't punish me. She would just give me her advice and a biblical anecdote. She simply said her piece and left it at that. I usually half-listened and did the "Yeah, yeah whatever" routine. I remember telling her that we were not in the olden days anymore and that times had changed.

But somewhere in my subconscious mind, the things she told me stuck. Not because she beat me over the head and forced me to sit down and listen to her. No. Her message was more powerful because she said what she had to say and then left it at that. She didn't make me wrong for the choices I made, nor did she repeatedly remind me of how right she was. She didn't have to remind me. Because every time I messed up, I found myself thinking about all the advice and encouragement she'd given me.

It was those simple little things.

She would say, "Don't let the left shoe know what the right shoe is doing."

Or "Everybody ain't your friend."

Or "Keep your enemies close to you."

Or "Stop following folks and be your own leader."

Or "Walk with your head up high."

My grandmother often encouraged me. "Leave this city and go to college, because there isn't anything here. Explore the world."

When I asked questions about God, she said, "Look into other religions. Explore everything. Learn as much as you can. Ask questions if you don't know something."

When I felt down or upset over something someone had said, my grandmother was right there. "Don't let anyone tell you what you can't do," my grandmother encouraged me.

But the most important thing she told me that I hold dearly to this day was, "I didn't raise you like that."

She was absolutely right. She didn't raise me like that. I knew better.

So whenever I was out in the streets doing something I knew I shouldn't be doing, I would hear my grandmother's voice in the background. Even when I did decide to do something wrong anyway, she always let me learn on my own. She knew I had to get the hard knocks from life. She couldn't save me from everything.

I appreciate all those things she told me.

When I got older, I was able to fully understand all her wisdom and advice. I have been fortunate enough to be able to tell her many times how much I appreciated those talks and golden words of love. They have sustained me in my life, relationships, career, and friendships.

As your Gay Best Friend, ladies, I am here to tell you that as much as you may know something for sure, and as much as you may be right, there are some things men have to do and learn on their own.

I know it's hard to stand by and watch someone go through something you may know is not right. It's difficult to see someone fall.

But gospel singer Donnie McClurkin said it best. "We fall down, but we get up."

## Chapter 18

# Money Can Buy Sex, but Not Love:
# Gigolos Get Lonely Too

The lack of judgment some women exercise when it comes to men and money amazes me. I don't know if it's the sweet talk in your ears at night, or the over-the-top sex that leaves you begging for more, or because you hate to see a "good" brother down. Whatever the reasons, I have met *too* many women who have shared stories of how they were left with bad credit after dating a man, and the mind-boggling amount of money they spent trying to keep that man.

I want you to think about something for a moment. If a woman allows a man whom she's not much interested in dating to wine and dine her, buy her trinkets, jewelry, pay her rent, and splurge on trips, then that woman is (rightly) called a gold-digger or a prostitute. Now, if the roles are reversed and a man does the same thing to a woman, what should we call him? Yup, you guessed it. A gigolo, or a pimp.

Spending money on a man will not make him fall in love with you. It will not guarantee that he will be faithful to you. Nor will it guarantee that you are in a real relationship with him. You may be in *some* kind of relationship, but it's a financial or sexual one, not one based on true feelings, love, or his respect for you.

If your man asks for money after you have sex ("Hey, baby, can I get a few dollars? I need to take care of some things"), then he is a gigolo. If every time he calls you it's because he is in a bind and he really needs your help ("My car is acting up," "I need to pay some bills," or "My rent is late. Can you help me out?"), you guessed it again. He is a gigolo. He is pimping you for your money.

You, Diva-cakes, work *too damn hard and long* for your money. Why would you give it away to some man because you feel if you don't the relationship will end? Why aren't you paying your *own* bills or your tithes? How about *you* take care of *you* and let *him* figure out how to get out of his own predicament? He got himself in it. Let him be smart, man, and wise enough to get out of it. He is an adult. A grown-ass man. Hell, point him toward some money management classes on how to manage his finances. You are not a bank, an ATM, a credit-lender, or a member of the FDIC.

A man who will sit at home and not work is a man who needs to be out on the streets. If he is not helping you by contributing financially to the household in any way, give him the boot. Put him out and let him go live with his mother, where *she* can baby and care for him. You are not his mother. You are his woman. And you are definitely not a caregiver for an able-bodied man who can go to work and earn a living.

I can hear some of you now.

"The economy is bad and he has been unable to find work."

Or "He is in between jobs. He needs help to get back on his feet."

Girl, I am giving it to you straight from your Gay Best Friend. I understand the economy is bad. I even can understand he is in between jobs and needs some help getting back on his feet. But if you have been waiting on him to get a job and it's been over a year, I'm sorry, he's got to go. If he is not out every day pounding the pavement, scouring the Internet, or attending job fairs, but laying on the sofa playing video games, watching television all day, and eating all the food in the house? Nope. No. *Hell, no!*

Put him out. Today is the last day. It is over. Done. Finished.

No more living off the fat of the land. *Your* land. It's time to hand out a notice: *Your services are no longer needed. This is effective immediately. You. Have. Got. To. Go. Now!*

Now, ladies, you are going to flip your wigs and lace-fronts when I tell you this next story. It even took me a minute to recuperate after hearing it.

A good friend of mine, "Vivian," is a fierce woman! (You notice I put an exclamation point there. It's because she is.)

Vivian is an Ivy-league graduate. She drives a BMW and lives in a condo in New Jersey. She owns her own multi-million-dollar business and due to her success, she has been a commentator on television shows offering business advice for entrepreneurs.

Vivian is fly! She's stylish and chic. Her beautiful skin radiates with a natural glow. And don't get me started on her culinary skills. Vivian can cook her *behind* off. The brunches and dinners at home should be featured on the Food Network.

Vivian has it going on. She is a class act. She is a Diva.

One afternoon we were having brunch in Vivian's condo and she sullenly said to me, "Terrance, I really need to talk with you about something." I noticed the pain in her voice and it shocked me. I have never known Vivian to be bothered by anything, so I said, "Sure. What is it?"

Vivian sat at the dining room table across from me and she took a deep breath.

"I don't know who to talk to about this." She looked over at me.

I knew it was serious, because I've never known her to have a problem she couldn't find a way to figure out. "Vivian, you know you can talk to me about anything," I said.

"Well, you know, 'David' and I have been seeing one another for a little over a year."

Okay, ladies, before we continue, let me give you a little back-story on David. He is a comedian. Well, a *struggling* comedian. He's done some major gigs across the country, and he hosts a comedy club on the weekends. But he doesn't work a day job, because he decided to dedicate himself to his comedy full-time. Every time I've met David, he's always nice and smiling, and he appears to love Vivian.

Now, let's get back to Vivian's story. "So David and I have been seeing one another for a little over a year. However, I'm starting to think if the relationship has run its course and I'm not sure if I want to invest any more time, energy, or money into it."

You *know* my ears perked up when I heard the money part.

"What do you mean?" I asked.

"You know David is an aspiring comedian," Vivian said. I nodded my head. "Well, I am trying very hard to be the supportive girlfriend and be there for him, but it's really becoming a strain. He doesn't work. His gigs are few and far between."

"But doesn't he host the comedy club and make money?" I asked curiously.

"He's not making a lot of money from that," Vivian said and shook her head. "It all depends on how many people come through door. If there isn't a large crowd, then he doesn't make a lot of money, if any at all."

"I see," I said. "So, continue."

"Well, every time I have to go out of town on business, David comes along at my expense. I pay for his airfare, hotel, and meals while we are out of town." Vivian picked up her glass of wine and took a sip. "Even when we are here and we go out to dinner, I have to pick up the tab. He never pays for anything. The movies, outings, and concerts are all out of my pocket."

I picked up my glass of wine and took a big gulp.

"When we decide to get together at my home after work, I have to drive all the way to Brooklyn, pick him up, and then drive all the way back to New Jersey. That is very taxing. I am so *tired* after work."

"Why can't he take the train to Jersey and meet you?" I asked.

"He doesn't like taking the train."

"What about the bus?"

Vivian sucked her teeth and rolled her eyes. "He won't take the bus."

I took another big gulp of my wine.

"But I have more." Vivian stared at me with tears forming in her eyes.

"What is it? It's okay," I said and moved closer to her.

"For the past year I have been paying David's rent," Vivian said.

"*Excuse me?*" I said.

"I have been paying his rent for a year," Vivian repeated. "I give him the money each month to pay his rent."

"How much is his rent?" I asked.

"It's twelve hundred dollars," Vivian said.

My face dropped and my mouth fell open.

"And you know what, Terrance? I have never been inside his house. I don't even know what it looks like inside."

That was *it*. I had to stop Vivian. I couldn't take it anymore. It was time for me to let loose and read Vivian the riot act.

"Wait a minute. Let me get this straight. You have been paying David's rent, which is twelve hundred dollars, for a year, and you don't know what his apartment looks like inside? So when you go to pick him up why don't you go knock on the door and go inside?" I said.

"He won't let me come in. I have to call him from outside and let him know I am there."

"Girl, no! You have to end this relationship *today*," I said. I wanted to throw my glass across the room. "You have been paying the *rent* on his *apartment* and he won't let you *inside*. Girlfriend, please, that is not his apartment. That is *your* apartment. You're the one paying the rent on it, so you have a *right* to go inside. And wait a minute, Ms. Honey. How do you know he doesn't live with another woman? How do you know it is his apartment? Hell, how do you even know he is paying the rent? He could be pocketing your money."

I was livid. I couldn't believe my friend, the Diva, an Ivy-league graduate who is intelligent, and runs her own company, was letting a man live off her, and she had no say in the relationship.

"I was trying to be the supportive girlfriend. I love him and wanted him to know I was there for him."

I sucked my teeth and wanted to sucker punch Vivian in the face.

"There isn't that much love in the world," I said. "He is using you and he's getting away with it. He is a gigolo. It's time to get rid of him and let him learn how to earn his own money from his comedy. You can be supportive, but not supportive financially. Especially paying his rent when you've never stepped foot in his apartment. Girl, I can't let that go."

Vivian heard me loud and clear, because a few weeks later she called to tell me that she ended the relationship with David.

"I just needed someone to give me confirmation of what I already knew," she said.

Many of you are in Vivian's shoes. You are caring for, supporting, and financially keeping a man, yet you are afraid if you stop, he will stop loving you.

Divas, he isn't loving you anyway. He is loving what you can do for him. That is not love. That is not care and concern for you, or your well-being. He is a pimp.

Stop giving your money away to him for some loving, his time, and his company.

You can buy yourself a puppy.

A man who will live off a woman is not a man at all. He is a leech, a mooch. He is lazy and trifling. You don't need that in your life. You have too much to worry about other than a man sitting in your house when you get home from work who hasn't cleaned the house, cooked, or even run a bath for you. (That is the *least* he can do if he is not going to work. He can take care of the home while you're working and bringing home the cash.)

I understand it may be hard for you to get rid of him because you may have committed to supporting him. You may have told him that you had his back and would be there for him. Not like the other people in his life who have turned on him and stopped believing in him and his dream.

Please, girl. Tell him to get a tangible dream and not a pipe dream.

Don't get me wrong. I am all for supporting someone and his dream, whatever it is, but if he is not doing anything to make his dream a reality, then he needs to awaken from his dream and get a job.

There is no excuse. Stop taking those sorry excuses from him.

Today is the day you will say, "I am not accepting the sad stories and pitiful excuses. I don't want to hear that nobody is hiring, or 'I've put in applications everywhere and no one has called me back.' It's time for you to be a man. So until you're ready to be a man and pull your weight, you have to go. I am not a bank, an ATM, or a money machine. It ends today."

Doesn't that sound wonderful? Doesn't that make you feel powerful and strong?

Girl, I know *I* feel much better.

Stop letting men use you. Don't be desperate and think you need to give a man money to be in a relationship with you. The first time a man asks to borrow some money, let that be a clue. The second time it happens, then it's a clear sign. The third time it happens, it's time to end the relationship. Sorry, that is the end of the line.

Take your money and go do something for you instead. Hit up the mall. Go to the spa. Travel to a foreign destination. Whatever you do, do something with the money that you earned. It's yours, and yours to take care of you.

The man for you—the one who has a job and a bank account—will show up and *want* to take you out. He will *want* to splurge on you. He won't even let you go into your purse and pull out any cash.

Don't you love the sound of that?

Good. Now go out, enjoy yourself and live abundantly, fiercely, and fabulously without a man riding your Donna Karan, Chanel, or Valentino coattails. You paid too much for your fashion to ruin it with a no-good trifling lazy man.

That is an ugly accessory.

# Chapter 19

# Yes, Girl, He Is Into You— And Him, Too!

Man, I swear that nearly every woman I know has lost her mind after J. L. King's book *On the Down Low* dropped a few years ago. It sparked a hail-storm of controversy within the black community, and scared the hell out of black women. And for good reason.

Down-low behavior, however, is nothing new to the gay community. It was (and is) something we have always been familiar with—men who sleep with men but who also have wives and girl-friends who would never suspect they also have sex with men.

Before I delve into this chapter, I would like to first remove the term "down-low" from our dialogue, because when people hear it, they think of black men. For one thing, it is naïve to think that black men are the only ones who are secretly having sex with other men. White, Spanish, Asian, and other cultures do it too. But when the term is commonly used, it is generally (and inappropriately) directed only toward black men. "Down-low" has a negative connotation and, unfortunately, makes all black men out to be predators.

Second, the original use of the term *down-low* described a secret affair. R&B singer R. Kelly had a popular song titled "Down Low (Nobody Has to Know)" about a heterosexual extramarital affair.

Third, the correct term to use is "men who have sex with men," or MSM. The Centers for Disease Control concluded in their studies that men who had sex with men did not identify as gay or bisexual, but rather as men with wives or girlfriends who frequently (or infrequently) have sex with other men.

Whew! That was a mouthful. But you ladies got it? Good. Now let's move on.

In my distant past, all I *ever* slept with were men who had wives or girlfriends. Even when I had girlfriends, I had sex with men on the side. Yup, I was confused about my sexuality. Yup, it was wrong to be in relationships with women and not tell them about my sexuality. I struggled to be in a monogamous relationship with a woman. I did have a few serious one-on-one relationships with women, hoping that it would be my cure, my way of leaving my secret life. I wrote all about it in *Hiding in Hip Hop*. Fortunately, I've now grown out of that behavior. I no longer sleep with men who have girlfriends and wives. That is a game I choose not to play. Today I find it appalling for a man to deceive and lie to a woman about his sexuality and use her as some type of scapegoat.

I also understand how it feels to hide your sexuality, because I grew up in the black church, and every Sunday I listened to my pastor preach emphatically that homosexuality is a sin. I tried to repress my sexual urges for men, but the more I prayed and denied myself, the more I yearned for the touch and feel of a man. And while the minister yelled and screamed from the pulpit about the sins of homosexual men, he made it appear that somehow, the act of homosexuality was far much worse than any other sin. (I found out years later, as an adult, that no one sin is greater than the other. And we all live in sin.)

I've also learned that there are many more men who have sex with men than I knew. I thought I was in a bubble, along with the men I was sleeping with. It was just us, no other men like us. But then an explosion happened and the cover was blown. Men who secretly have sex with other men are everywhere.

Since *Hiding in Hip Hop* was released, I am often asked by women if there is some look, sign, or dress that men who have sex with men share to identify one another. And I am always asked if it's something in the eyes, because that is what author J. L. King said during his appearance on *The Oprah Winfrey Show*.

Unfortunately, there is not.

There is no secret code or word, and definitely nothing in the eyes that will reveal a closeted man to another. So, emphatically, no! For the record, there is nothing that I can pinpoint as a significant indicator of how men who have sex with men identify one another.

However, I *can* share that the same signs of a man cheating in a heterosexual relationship are the same signs of him sleeping with another man. A man cheating is a man cheating. He will exhibit the same behaviors regardless of whom it's with.

As your Gay Best Friend, I will share some things that will make you go *hmmm* and wonder if he's creeping with another man.

Okay, ladies, here we go. First, men who have sex with men are very good deceivers. Better yet, they are *exceptional* liars. They know what to say, when to say it, and how to say it. They can string a woman along and make her feel like she is a queen. But if you are smart and savvy, you can spot and see through the lies and deception. For example, if your man begins to introduce you to a slew of men every other week (or month), none of whom you ever met before, and these new "buddies" never seem to be around after two or three months, then you should start to question these relationships.

You have a right to know. Ask your man what happened to his new friends and why they never come around anymore. There has to be a reason for the abrupt ending of the friendships. Ask why he stopped bringing them around.

Now, there are a couple of reasons he introduced his new friend to you in the beginning. One, the guy may appear to be extremely masculine, with no effeminate overtones. Your man may be very comfortable with his friend and may want to show him his world—especially his girl. Also, he knows that by introducing his friend to you (because women want to know who their men are hanging with), you would never suspect the guy of being gay and your man of sleeping with him. Two, he is trying to make you feel comfortable with his undercover boyfriend. He will introduce him to you because when he says he's out with his boy, you will not give any thought as to what they are doing (and whether they are doing "it" together).

Second, a man who has sex with other men will have multiple e-mail accounts and possibly a second cell phone, and he will know your schedule like clockwork. I've been with men who tell me, "My girl is going to be at work this weekend. Let's hook up then." I've also been with these men when their woman has called. "Hey baby," he says. "Yeah, I'm just chilling right now." I am sitting right next to him while she thinks her man is home alone.

Ladies, I am not a fan of snooping around, but you have a right to investigate if you suspect him of dipping out on you. When you log onto the computer and you see several different screen names, he's hiding something from you. (Especially if one of those screen names is *dl4u, topman4bottom,* or *discreetdude.* Those are dead giveaways.) Check the cookies or the history on the computer. This is easy to do. When you check the history on the computer it will bring up all the websites he's visited, and you will know if he's been to gay websites like adam4adam.com or blackgaychat.com looking for a sex hookup.

If you notice a second cell phone and you don't have the number for it, he is *definitely* hiding something from you. But more important, if your gut instincts tell you something is not right, then it probably isn't.

Third, I tell women you have to *ask* a man if he is sleeping with another man. I learned that from one closeted man I was sleeping with. When his girlfriend accused him of cheating, he denied it emphatically. He told me, "She keeps accusing me of cheating. Well, she got the cheating part right, but she keeps asking, 'Who is she?' She is not asking the right question."

That is when I learned that if you don't ask a man the right question, you will not get the right answer.

So you have to be specific. If you suspect you may be dating a man who sleeps with men, ask him, "Have you *ever* had sex with another man?"

The question you *don't* want to ask is, "Are you sleeping with another man?" That is an accusatory question. You don't want to accuse him. If you do, he will deny it. Trust me, a down-low man will never admit to sleeping with another man, especially to his woman. You will have to catch him in the act, and it won't be easy. But if you ask him, "Have you *ever* had sex with another man?" that leaves the question open to previous experiences. Hopefully your man will be forthright in revealing any of his encounters.

Still, I seriously doubt it.

Fourth, another sign is when your man introduces new sexual positions, especially anal sex, and wants to have a dildo inserted inside him. Don't be afraid to ask where he learned or saw this. I am sure he did not wake up one day and decide he wanted to try it. No. He has done this before. Sure, he may be a freak, and into all sorts of kinky things, but you should question these behaviors. I wrote more about this in *Hiding in Hip Hop*.

I want to tell you something, girlfriend, don't do anything you are uncomfortable doing, especially if you have concerns about his sexuality. Your love for him is not based on the type of sex you are willing or unwilling to engage in. Love and protect yourself. It's your body and your life.

Last, don't be afraid to speak up and say something. You are more important than you may think. Having a man in your life is great, but if you have questions and speculations about his sexuality, new friends, and suspicious lifestyle, then you deserve it to yourself to be careful. Love life and, more important, love yourself.

Here is my story "Yes, Girl, He's Into You...And Him!" published on Essence.com, April 16, 2009:

*Shocked, appalled, flabbergasted, and simply outdone. That's the reaction many women had when resident gay hairstylist Dwight Eubanks of* The Real Housewives of Atlanta *fame announced his engagement to a woman.*

I must admit: I too was taken aback by his announcement. I'm a fan of the show and love Dwight's advice and friendship with NeNe. I personally feel every woman needs a Gay Best Friend. It's a necessity, just like a pair of Manolo Blahnik pumps. Besides, I respect the fact that Dwight is an openly gay man who has no qualms about his sexuality.

So, like many of you, I thought, *Why is he getting married to a woman?*

But then I thought, *Why is this woman marrying an openly gay man? Can't she find a man?*

Reality quickly stepped in and I reflected on something I shared in *Hiding in Hip Hop*. There are lots of men who have "cover girls," or the term you may be familiar with, "beards." These women knowingly date and marry men who are bisexual or gay. Yes, there are women who have no problem being in romantic or sexual relationships with men who sleep with other men. I saw quite a bit of it in the entertainment business. These women know what they are getting themselves involved in, and the terms and conditions of the relationships.

But it doesn't stop there. I met prominent men outside of entertainment—ministers, doctors, politicians, and businessmen. These men also have arranged relationships where the women are aware of the men's sexual desires.

Before you begin gasping, clutching your pearls, and throwing holy water, close your mouth and breathe. Ladies, you might be alarmed if you knew the number of women who are in relationships with men who have sex with other men.

Why do they do it? The reasons vary. They enjoy the companionship. They get the best of both worlds—a friend and a partner with whom they can talk, have fun, and appreciate the company. The relationship may provide financial stability. It could be for convenience. The list goes on and on. The point is, these women are perfectly happy.

For the record, not all relationships are based on sex. True, sex helps a relationship, but in an arranged situation such as these, it may not be important for either party. They both could be looking for something more meaningful. It's great to have it all, but let's be real—all relationships do not have over-the-top, climbing-the-walls, earth-shattering sex. (You would probably be amazed by the large number of sexless marriages.)

The reason a lot of these women keep their arranged relationships secret is simple. Just look at the comments made on the Internet about Dwight's announcement. I was alarmed by the number of women who responded with resentment and hatred toward Dwight. They vilified, crucified, and cursed him for entering into a relationship with a woman.

Whatever your sentiments may be toward Dwight, the fact remains that many women are uncomfortable with gay men. Yes, I said it. Many of you have hang-ups. You don't mind having a gay male friend and someone you can kee-kee with. It's okay when it's another woman's man or child who's gay. But when it hits home, you have a meltdown.

I hear women say all the time, "Why don't these down-low and closeted men just come out and say something?" What bothers me is that many women say they want to know the truth, but can they really handle the truth? Do they really want to know?

A lot of people were upset with me that I didn't disclose names in my book. They felt I was keeping those people in the closet and protecting them. But my book isn't about outing celebrities. It is about my personal journey and experience of coming to terms with my sexuality and the difficulty I faced.

Don't get me wrong. I agree with a lot of you that a bisexual or gay man should stay in his lane. Don't involve women. If you are deceiving and lying to women, you should stop it. Be honest and let the woman make a choice whether she wants to be involved in a relationship with a man who has sex with other men.

Dwight boldly told his fiancée his truth. He revealed to her his sexuality and allowed her the opportunity to make a choice in the matter.

What he did is something a lot of down-low and closeted men could never do. Hell, he did something many heterosexual men who cheat on their girlfriends and wives *with women* could never do. Dwight's actions proved his manhood. He's honest from the beginning. He didn't hide, deny, or say he was delivered from being gay. His fiancée knows what she is getting. It is her choice and her option to stay in the relationship. She has the power to do what she feels is best for her.

You say you want honesty?

Well, now you got it.

Yet, when the man is too honest you still point the judgmental finger.

So, ask yourself: What is it that you really want?

# Worksheets

# Know Better, Do Better

**Scenario 1**

You have been in a relationship with your boyfriend for two years. Everything is going great, despite the occasional lows you experience. (Hey, who doesn't have low moments in their relationship, right?)

One day while cleaning the house, you discover a card with another woman's name and number on it. The discarded business card is not from a place you recognize. You chalk it up as nothing major. You will ask him about it later when he comes home from work.

When your man comes home and you confront him about the card, he says got it from a vendor when he was walking down the street. She was selling some of her products and she gave him her card. No big deal.

A few weeks later, you notice that he steps out of the room when his cell phone rings. His voice lowers during these conversations and he always appears to be angry or upset after the calls.

You ask what the problem is. He tells you that it's nothing.

You pry a little more and he tells you that it was his boss, or one of his boys calling about something insignificant.

A month later you, get a phone call from a woman who tells you that your boyfriend is the father of her six-month-old child. She has been seeing him for over a year and she knows all about you.

Unfortunately, you know nothing about her.

You refuse to believe her. The last time your boyfriend cheated, several months into the beginning of your relationship, he promised he would never let it happen again.

You confront him over the phone at his job. He denies it and tells you that he will talk with you when he gets home.

You anxiously wait for him to get home. You can't wait until he walks through that door. After all you've done for him, you can't believe that he has stepped out on you again and got some heifer pregnant.

You lunge at him as soon as he comes through the door. He pulls you off of him. You keep swinging and cursing at him. He tells you to calm down so he can explain. You sit down on the sofa breathing hard and heavy. He sits next to you.

He grabs your hand and strokes it. He hugs you and kisses you. He tells you that he is sorry. He confesses to his infidelities. He didn't mean for it to happen. She was just some chick he met and she doesn't mean anything to him. He tells you that you are his world, his everything. He wants you to accept his apology.

*What do you do?*

A. Look at him square in his face, slap the mess out of him, and tell him to pack all his belongings and get the hell out.

B. Tell him you love him too, and that he is your world and your everything. You are going to stand by his side and help him through this dilemma.

C. First, you forgive yourself for getting yourself in this mess, because the first time he cheated, you should have left. Secondly, you forgive *him* because he only did what you allowed him to do. When there were no repercussions for his behavior the first time, he felt he could do it again and you would take him back just like you did the first time. Third, you forgive the woman he got pregnant, because her low self-esteem allowed her to sleep with another woman's man without any consideration for all involved. Last, you end the relationship and tell him to be a man and take care of his responsibility without you. You let him know that you deserve better and that you love yourself way too much to allow someone to mistreat or misuse you in any way.

### Scenario 2

It's been six months since you've seriously dated or been in a relationship with a man. Since you've read this book, you decided to go ahead and ask God for the type of you man you need.

You sat down and compiled your list. You described to a T the type of man you need.

Guess what? A few weeks later you were at the grocery store when you saw the man from your list. You became flustered. He smiled at you. You smiled back. He came over to you and you could feel yourself about to melt.

He is six-foot-three, dark, bald-headed, Mandingo type of brother. He looks like the model Tyson with a little street edge. He's a professional brother who has risen above his hard background growing up in the projects with a single mother. He's loving, caring, compassionate, and sexy as all get out.

For the next couple of months, things were going great. He treated you like a lady. He paid for the dates. He surprised you with flowers delivered to your office.

But.

You haven't slept with him and you are wondering why. You want him badly. It's been six months since you've been with a man. Your body is yearning for some TLC and Abdul is just the man to take care of it.

Abdul. What a minute. Isn't that a Muslim name?

Yes, Abdul was born and raised a Muslim. He prays five times a day. He doesn't eat pork. He doesn't drink alcohol or smoke, anything.

He is not having sex with a woman until he's married.

You panic.

You are really feeling Abdul. You are a Christian woman, born and raised. Even though you know you're supposed to wait until you are married to have sex, you are guilty of fornicating in the past. You justified it by telling yourself, "You've got to try out the goods before you get married. You don't want to be disappointed if you're not sexually compatible."

But now Abdul tells you that he will only marry a Muslim woman. You are a Christian.

You go back to your list to review what you wrote. Surprise! You didn't include religion. You didn't think about spirituality. You assumed that because you were a Christian woman you would meet a Christian man.

*What do you do?*

A. Tell Abdul you will convert to the Muslim faith. You don't want to lose him. He is the man of your dreams and you couldn't imagine him with any woman other than you.

B. Tell Abdul that you are a Christian woman. Let him know it was great getting to know him, but it would be a waste of both your time to continue, because you are not converting religions for a man. Then, you go back to your list and include religion as something that matters to you.

C. Try to convince him that he should convert to Christianity.

**Scenario 3**

You are at church. One of the members is always nice to you. He goes out of his way to speak to you every time he sees you. He's attractive, taller than you, and his appearance is decent. You are not floored, but you like the attention.

He asks you out on a date. You accept. He picks you up in his 1998 Honda Accord. You drive a brand-new G6 Infiniti. He brings you a rose. You smile, because it's the thought that counts.

Your date is movies and then dinner. While at the movies he asks if you would like anything. You say sure. You would like a soda. He comes back with a small soda for you. He has nothing for himself.

After the movie, he drives to Family House restaurant, the all-you-can-eat buffet in the strip mall. Your initial response is shock. Reality sets in. Yes, he has brought you to an all-you-can-eat buffet in a strip mall.

During dinner, you barely touch your food. He has already had two servings and making his way for a third. But he makes great conversation and makes you laugh. He compliments you through-out dinner. You like that. Despite the food disaster, you make it through the date and make plans for another.

The next date is to the zoo. It's buy-one-ticket-get-the-other-half-off day. You are the half-off.

The third date is to the museum. Saturday morning he picks you up. The weekends are free at the museum.

You discover that after waiting in line for forty-five minutes.

And now, a few months have gone by. You absolutely adore him. He has stepped up his game and you can't imagine not being without him. He has all the qualities you are looking for except for one flaw.

He is cheap as all get-out. The man doesn't want to spend money on anything.

*What do you do?*

A.  Tell him to beat it. You ain't no five-and-dime trick. You need a man who is willing to spend his dough, especially on you.

B.  Analyze the situation. He is by far one of the most amazing men you have met in a while. You are not willing to give up so soon on this relationship. You decide to be honest and have a conversation with him about money. You let him know how you really feel about him. You let him know in a lovingly manner how you would like to be treated, wined, and dined. Hey, you never know, he may be the man for you and be willing to spend a little more.

C.  Decide that if he is not going to spend his money, then you definitely will not be spending yours. Then you plot to invade his bank account, because you know he has big money. Any man that cheap must be saving his money.

## Scenario 4

You have been meaning to go back to college to get your degree, but you just don't have the time. You've been in your job as an assistant for three years. You want to move on, but you don't think you can do it. Especially with Tracey around, who seems to have it all together. You can't stand Tracey. She gets on your last nerve. She's always taking your shine in meetings, and you don't think you can compete with her on the education level.

You don't dress the way you like for work, because you think you are too fat. You are constantly telling yourself that you have to lose at least twenty-five pounds.

You don't like having sex with your boyfriend because he fancies Janet Jackson and Halle Berry. Your body certainly doesn't compare to those women's bodies.

You call your mother, who is no support at all. She reminds you how fat you are and tells you that you can't keep eating all those sweets you crave. She knows because she used to feed them to you as a child. She watched you grow out of your body into the woman you are. The extra weight you have gained over the years has not pushed you over the fat zone, but you think you are there.

You call your sister and best friend. They encourage you through you umpteenth diet phase.

Your boyfriend tells you that you are fine. He loves your body. You don't believe him, because it seems that all your ex-boyfriends have girlfriends that are your ideal weight.

After three months of dieting, you've only lost five pounds. You can't take it any longer so you stop dieting. Again.

Your boyfriend wants to start having sex in the daytime and with the lights on.

Your mom, yet again, reminds you that you need to stop eating so much before you lose your man.

*What do you do?*

A. You agree with your mother. Mothers know best. You are overweight and you don't want to lose your man. Besides, all you have to do is commit yourself to the diet this time— really commit—and it won't fail. You keep finding excuses to have sex with your boyfriend with the lights off.

B. You tell your mother to kiss your black behind. She's just as fat as you. Then you dump your boyfriend. How dare he ask you to have sex with the lights on, especially when he knows that you are not comfortable with your body?

C. Say a little prayer for yourself. Go to the mirror and affirm yourself. Tell all the parts of your body that you love them. Tell yourself that you are sorry for mistreating you, and forgive you. Let your boyfriend know that you love him and you agree with him. You do have a *banging* body and there is absolutely nothing wrong with you. Start each morning affirming the love you have for yourself, and you will start loving everything about you.

**Scenario 5**

You have just starting seeing a man who is well educated, and has a *career*, not a job. He's smart, funny, witty, and easy to talk to. You enjoy his company and he enjoy yours.

You can tell he's not your typical brother. There is something definitely different about him. He has invited you to join him for an afternoon jazz concert in the park and then dinner at LeCirque, the new trendy restaurant on the rich side of town.

The only thing you know about jazz is Wynton Marsalis and Miles Davis. You don't even listen to the music. You like some old-school R&B and a little hip-hop.

You don't mind trying new things, but this brother is definitely a connoisseur of the finer things. You are a connoisseur of sorts, but you have different tastes. There is nothing wrong with that, but this brother is right on the money and you are feeling his vibe.

The following week, he invites you to join him for a wine tasting up north. Afterward, he wants to check out a new art exhibit at the museum.

These activities are amazing. You are learning a lot. It's totally different from your experiences with other men you have dated. He's a different caliber.

Unfortunately, the more he invites you out, the more uncomfortable you become. He's definitely a great guy, but the conversation is hard to maintain because you are not as savvy or educated about these new experiences as he is. He is a great conversationalist and he likes teaching you about these things, but how long can you be the student?

Besides, every time he invites you out, it's a huge task finding the right thing to wear. You are not sure about the attire for these events. You don't want to underdress or overdress. Ugh!

*What do you do?*

A.  Just give up and move on. You're not really missing anything. Most of the places he takes you are filled with nothing but bourgeois people anyway. Besides, he probably thinks he's better than you.

B.  Fake it. He won't suspect anything. You're good at making people believe what they want. He will never suspect that you are not as educated as he thinks. Besides, you know enough to get by anyway.

C.  You tell him the truth. You are not that informed on a lot of these experiences, but you are determined to learn as much as you can. On your own, you check out various workshops and classes that are offered at the community center or the community college. You start exploring other activities and events. You go to the library and brush up on your knowledge on them. The two of you make a great couple. You can also teach *him* a few things he is not informed about.

## Scenario 6

You have been in a relationship with your man for a number of years. You live together. You are settled into your relationship and you know him like the back of your hand. As he does you. There is nothing he can do or say that will catch you off guard. You know exactly what he will say and do at any given moment.

You have a few gripes with him, but you say nothing about them. You just work around the situation, because you know he is not going to change.

One problem is that he is always late for everything. He always has an excuse about why he can never make it on time. This has been irking you for some time now, and you have even started lying to him, giving him earlier start times for events. If they really start at six o'clock, you tell him four-thirty. If it's eight o'clock, you tell him six-thirty.

Also, he never answers his cell phone when he is out with his boys. He always has an excuse. He can't hear it. He leaves it in the car. It's always one thing or another. Although these are small things that annoy you, there is a larger problem looming.

During your time together, you have grown tremendously. You went back to school and got your degree. You received a promotion at your job and are now making more money than your boyfriend. You are tired of the apartment and want to move out of the city. A nice house in the suburbs is what you've been dreaming about since you moved in with your boyfriend.

For the past several months, you have been looking at homes and gathering information. You've started attending homeownership workshops—without him. You've also inquired about a loan.

Unfortunately, he has no desire to leave the city. As a matter of fact, he doesn't want to move too far from his job, family, or friends. He is perfectly content.

*What do you do?*

A. Force him to move with you. Tell him you will cover all the expenses. You will pay the movers, pay the mortgage, and even cook every day, despite the hour-and-a-half commute each way.

B. Go out, buy the house, and tell him about it afterward. That way he has no choice but to move to the suburbs. Besides, he doesn't know what's best for him anyway.

C. Lovingly sit down with him and let him know what's going on. Be honest about everything and how it makes it you feel. Let him know that you value his input and would like to work it out with a cooperative agreement. Investing in a new home will be a detriment to neither of you. In fact, you let him know how much of an investment it is.

## Scenario 7

Can a man actually be that fine, smart, and churchgoing? Something has to be wrong with him. He is all up in your grill. Smiling, flirting, getting you all hot and bothered.

Okay. You tell yourself that you will stop staring into his beautiful brown eyes.

His smile is warm and inviting. His body, from what you can tell in his T-shirt and jeans, is slamming. He has muscles all over.

He's perfect.

You ask him if he has a girlfriend. He tells you that he is not seeing anyone seriously. You ask what does that mean. He says he has some female friends that he's cool with. You ask again, what does "cool with" mean. They are just friends he chills with every now and then.

He takes you out on various dates and you happen to come across one of the "friends" he is chilling with. There is a confrontation between them. She asks who you are. You just sit back and watch the madness unfold.

He tells you that she is obsessive and controlling. He hates women who just don't take a hint. He is not looking for another crazy chick.

You immediately let him know that you are not like that, and he doesn't have to worry about you acting out on him. You can see why some women can get strung out on him. He is fine as all get-out.

As you two continue to get to know one another, he lets you in on another one of his habits. He tells you about an ex-girlfriend who was too demanding and accusatory. He couldn't do anything without her checking his cell phone, questioning him about his whereabouts, and jumping up in his face. He admits that he hit her a few times, but only because she deserved it. He had never put his hands on a woman before, but she always started the fight with him. He was only defending himself.

He tells you that he would never put his hands on you.

*What do you do?*

A. Let him know that are really feeling him and you are not concerned about the other women in his life. You are all the woman he needs. Besides, those other women did not have high self-esteem like you do. You are not a crazy, psycho and deranged woman.

B. Go through his cell phone, get the numbers of the other women, and call them up to find out what's really going on with them. Mama didn't raise no fool, and you definitely ain't going to let him pull the wool over your eyes.

C. You know that when people tell you who they are, you need to believe them. If he hit his ex, you know there is nothing that will prevent him from doing it to you. You definitely know what "we just cool" means. He is letting you know that you are definitely not the only woman he is seeing. You end the relationship and let him know that you are not desperate, lonely, or fearful, and you have no problem waiting for the right man to come along.

**Scenario 8**

Your friends set you up with a great guy they know you will like. He has a professional job. He lives alone, has no children, and is single. Knowing your friends, you are reluctant. They have good intentions, yet their taste is totally opposite of yours.

When you finally agree to this blind date, your nerves are on edge. You can't believe that your friends are doing this and you can't believe that you are doing this.

When you meet him at the restaurant you are totally blown away. You can't believe that your friends actually set you up with a good-looking man.

The dinner goes off without a hitch. You both agree to see one another again. You're excited that this is something that might be worth investing your time and energy in.

You have a second, third, fourth, and now a fifth date with him. It's going great. Nothing out of the ordinary stands out, except that he is very casual and laid back. He doesn't come off very aggressive like most men you've dated. As a matter of fact, he is *too* laid back. You've had sex with him a couple of times and it was great, but he hasn't said anything about where this relationship is going. You are curious to know, so you bring it up to him on the date.

He lets you know that he came out of a long-term relationship six months prior to meeting you. He really likes you and thinks you are a great person. He enjoys your company and especially the sex. He lets you know that he is not sure if he is ready for a relationship, but likes the way things are going with the two of you.

*What do you do?*

A. Let him know that you are fine with that, and that you enjoy his company too. You hope that something can happen between the two of you and would like to continue seeing him.

B. Excuse yourself from the table. Tell him that you have to go to the restroom and ditch him. Leave him sitting there. You can't believe that he didn't tell you sooner about his last relationship.

C. Be honest with yourself and him. Let him know that you are looking for a relationship and that he needs time to heal from his previous relationship. Let him know that you can be his friend, but sharing an intimate relationship with you at this time would not be wise for either of you.

## Scenario 9

You attend church regularly. As a matter of fact, you are there every Sunday. You are a faithful member and have been tithing and doing everything you are supposed to be doing as a Christian woman.

One of the men in the church is quite a catch. You haven't seen him attached to any woman. He is always respectful and polite to you.

One Sunday morning he approaches you and asks you out on a date. It takes you by surprise, but hey, he is a Christian man and there are no scandals lurking around him among the church folks.

He wines and dines like you've never been before. After a few dates and no sex, he tells you that he has something important to speak with you about. You are anxious and nervous. You wonder what could it be. You've been without a man for six months. You told yourself that you were going to wait for the right man to come along. You were not going to let another man distract you again.

He tells you that he has been praying for a woman like you. He feels that you are from God. He then proceeds to tell you that he heard from God that you are the woman from him. He has never gotten that feeling or word before. He has been saving himself for you. He really feels that you two are made for one another.

He then lets you know that he has two children with another woman. He has not seen his children in two years, because they live in another state. The mother of his children will not let them come visit him, and he is trying hard to get custody or visitation with them.

Although she left him, he lets you know that she was a terrible, nasty, mean woman. He can't stand her and he wishes he'd never met her.

He then tells you that he is working part-time but looking to start his own business and that he wants a strong woman who can stand by his side and help him realize his dream. He feels that you are that woman. He knows it—because you have a marketing degree, and you would be great to help him get his business off the ground.

*What do you do?*

A.  Tell him that you are not ready to make a commitment to anyone at this time. You are willing to take things slow with him and not rush into anything. You are still working on yourself spiritually, and if God spoke to him, you are sure that God will let you know, too, if he is the man for you. Also, you let him know that he needs to focus on one thing at a time. Either focus on his children he hasn't seen in two years or his business. Besides, you are not quite ready to invest in someone else's dream. You are still working on your dreams.

B.  Tell him you feel the same way. You know that he is the man for you and you feel where he is coming from. You know how women can be, especially when it comes to children. You think between the two of you, the business would be a great investment.

C.  Call all your friends to see what they think. Then pray and ask for guidance. You're still not sure what to do. No one can seem to give you any answers. Your friends sound jealous. God hasn't answered your prayers. So why not keep dating him and see where it goes? He just may be the man for you.

**Scenario 10**

You've been in a relationship with your boyfriend for a little over a year. Everything is going okay. It's just that he just can't seem to do anything right. Ever since you've been dating him, you have had to correct his behavior—especially what you like and don't like.

It seems no matter what he does, it annoys you to no end. You have to let him know how it aggravates you that you have to keep reminding him of what he is doing wrong.

Every time you get into an argument, he either walks away or tells you it won't happen again. Yet it does, and you find yourself repeating yourself.

You kept bugging him about your apartment that needed a new paint job. He agreed to paint your place. He comes over and attempts to paint your home with the colors you picked out. But once he starts, you let him know that he has already started doing it wrong. He didn't put enough paper down. He didn't cover the furniture. And why is he painting in the sweatshirt and jeans you bought him?

Moving forward, your boyfriend occasionally forgets certain dates or events. It's not intentional. He just doesn't remember things in detail. He also has made a few mistakes but heck, nobody's perfect.

*What do you do?*
A. Keep reminding him how wrong he is. If you don't correct him, he will never learn. You have invested a lot into this relationship and you are not going to let him make a fool out of you.
B. Just look at him like he's crazy every time he says something that doesn't make sense. You don't care if he wants to look like a fool. You keep your mouth closed and laugh at him behind his back.
C. Let him know you love him. It is not your intention to be malicious, mean, or spiteful when you are correcting or giving him advice. You let him know that some information he has is incorrect. You don't make it a point to point out all his wrongs. Let him know that you are not there to judge him. If he is not sure of anything he can feel free to ask you for your opinion or advice.

# Acknowledgments

I thank God for the blessings and gifts that have been bestowed upon me. I do not take for granted my gifts and opportunities. Without Him, none of this would be possible.

This book also wouldn't be possible without the wonderful and talented people who saw the vision, believed in the work, and knew this book made sense. They are:

My publisher/editor Doug Seibold—so many thanks to you. We finally got the opportunity to work together. Thank you for believing in me and this book. It means the world to me.

My fellow sistergirl editor, Denise Montgomery. You so rock. Thank you for your patience, time, and understanding.

And to all the Agate/Bolden family who have stepped in and made this experience such a beautiful and creative work. Thank you!

Now, for all those *Divas* and splendiferous women who make me better, smarter, and wiser:

Special thanks to the Bradford ladies—Tiffany, Kristine, Eboni, Sandrea, and my wonderful aunt, Priscilla. I love you ladies and I'm glad you're my family.

The sassy ladies of 3 Chicks on Lit (Nakea, Tiffany, TuShonda), Victoria Christopher Murray, Marva Allen and the HueMan Bookstore Family, Deborah Bennett and my Interactive One/ Hello Beautiful family. Thank you for allowing me to express myself each week with my advice column. I couldn't have done this without you!

Thank you to Nefertiti and The Truth Bookstore Family, Crystal Bobb-Semple and the Brownstone Books family, Andrea Collier, Yetta Young, Tina Andrews, Rochelle Riley, Janaya Black, my Fisk University family, and the classes of '91, '92, and '93.

Sabrina Lamb, Marcia Pendelton, Desiree Cooper, Deborah Gregory, Myra Panache, Paula Renfroe, Nikki Webber, Nicole Childers, the wonderful reviewers of APOOO, the Fabulous Divas of *Essence* and essence.com, Ms. Tamika Newhouse and African Americans on the Move Book Club, Nikkea Smithers and the Readers With Attitude Book Club.

A special shout-out to all the book clubs who've shown me love and supported me. I appreciate each of you and I'm looking forward to coming to your meetings. So you better send me an invitation!

And to all my friends on Facebook, Twitter, and Black Planet: I appreciate your comments, friend requests, and continued support.

To all the men (friends) in my life, and those who are newly introduced, I cannot thank you enough for your love and support. You all helped make this happen.

If I've forgotten anyone, group, or organization please forgive my heart. You all mean the world to me and know that you always have a gay best friend in me.